A little something
to remind you of your
time in CPS Press Office
and your part in the
"trial of the century"
 best wishes,
    Julie Seddon
August 2004

Soham:
A Story of Our Times

Soham:
A Story of Our Times

NICCI
GERRARD

✳ SHORT BOOKS

First published in 2004 by
Short Books
15 Highbury Terrace
London N5 1UP

10 9 8 7 6 5 4 3 2 1

A CIP catalogue record for this book
is available from the British Library.

ISBN 1-904095-92-5

Printed in Germany by
GGPMedia, Poessneck

Prologue

One damp August evening, in a small town in Cambridgeshire, two little girls wearing identical Manchester United football shirts went missing; they were never seen alive again.

Why did we care so very much? Why did Jessica Chapman and Holly Wells capture the heart of a nation, the headlines of every newspaper day after day, when all around us children go missing, children are hurt, children are killed; when there was a war coming grimly over the horizon; when famines and plagues were gripping entire countries? What made these two little girls become such ghosts to haunt us – whose search was a story we followed hour by hour (though of course we soon knew what its ending must be); whose village became a shrine of flowers rotting sweetly in cellophane, of soft toys with beadily staring eyes and of love-letters and prayers written out by hand and anguished, schmaltzy, tear-jerking goodbyes from strangers; whose death unleashed a great flood of sorrow from people who didn't weep at their own losses and regrets; whose individual tragedy became a modern fairytale, though without the fairytale consolations? Hansel and Gretel did not find their way home; the wolf did eat Red Riding Hood; the Babes were forever lost in the deep dark wood.

On the one hand was the emblematic death of innocence – the blonde 'angel' and the dark-haired 'tomboy' sucked out of their happy, ordinary lives, into the black hole of Ian Huntley's rage and desire. On the other was the horror at the heart of a very English town: the caretaker who did not take care, but was a predator stalking those he should have protected, a wolf in sheep's clothing. And raging all around, the frantic media and a great glut of sorrow and fear; a hysteria of caring, an addiction of empathy. The media at first fed the story but it soon became a forest fire, out of control and growing hot on rumour and pity. Our attention was focused on Holly Wells, Jessica Chapman and their parents, and later on the man with the beetle brow and anxious eyes who might have killed them, the girlfriend with a pale, crooked face who might have helped him. For a while, nothing else seemed to matter: we waited with the parents, day by day, through all the misdirections and the flare and fading of false hopes, until at last the naked bodies were found in a damp, nettle-filled ditch at the end of a hidden rutted lane, until at last the caretaker and his girlfriend were charged and taken away, and the waiting was over.

The fire didn't quite go out, though. It glowed through the following year, flickering into brighter life when fuelled by intermittent whispers and reports (body parts had been found, a wider paedophile ring was suspected and the double murder was only the dark core of a dark mystery, Huntley had said nothing, Huntley was mad, Huntley wasn't mad at all but only pretending, Maxine Carr was Myra Hindley mark two, Carr was standing by Huntley, Carr had broken off with Huntley, Huntley had tried to kill himself, Carr had tried to kill herself, the evidence against him was cast-iron, there was no evidence to speak of...). It blazed into life once more with the court case a year and a half later, which lasted many weeks and was reported in minute and almost pornographic detail. Sometimes the double-page spreads in newspapers resembled court transcripts.

On television news, the blank photographs of the police van delivering Huntley to court and taking him away again, or the parents walking from the Old Bailey, were repeatedly shown. Once again, we were transfixed by the unfolding story, and couldn't get enough of it. Hundreds of thousands of words, millions of words, were written and read. Like a certain kind of second-rate art, it gripped us tight, pressing all the right buttons. It had all the ingredients for a police procedural, a court drama, a whodunnit, a whydunnit, a tragedy, a morality tale, a heart-wrencher and a modern myth. It didn't have a happy ending but it had – this is a word that should be banned but was used over and again – *closure*. At the end of the trial Ian Huntley was led from the dock, out of the limelight and into the darkness; from the clamour of words into a silence. He's just one name now, among the role call of names that send a little shudder down our spines.

During the long, meticulous trial, we felt that we were about to get to the heart of the mystery – bit by bit, we were led over its threshold, out of the daylight of ordinary life and into the small house where we knew the girls had died, up the stairs, into the cramped bathroom, into the bedroom with its matching covers, even to the bed – but we never got there, to the dark heart, the convulsed mind, the actual moment, the still point when time stopped for Jessica Chapman and Holly Wells. How could we? Life isn't like that, neat and with one answer, one moment, an explanation that could tell us how and tell us why and label things neatly so: guilty, innocent, evil, good, and allow us to put it all away in a file marked 'Closed'. In this case, the more numerous the words, the further off was the sense that we actually understood.

We love stories, and need them. They feed a deep and enduring human instinct. We understand the world through the stories we tell about it. In the single narrative, we extrapolate wider meanings. One life will engage our personal sympathies while a whole plethora of statistics will not. We need to imagine what it's like, need to identify in order to properly care. Through stories, we impose patterns, make meanings, give beginnings and endings, because we can't bear a world or a self without them.

But there is a multitude of stories to choose from, and we take the ones that we want and ignore the others. Without a story, an event does not root itself into our imagination and thus shrivels and disappears. With it, an event is simplified, or even created. In our desire for narrative order, we shine our torch into the darkness and believe that what we see illuminated in its narrow circle of light can be called the truth, ignoring all that dwells outside it.

***

What was the lesson of Soham, its meaning and its 'truth'? In 1995 I sat through the seven-week trial of Rosemary West. Frederick and Rosemary West tortured their own children and tortured and murdered other people's children; their victims were objects of their murderous sexual pleasure: living sex aids and later, a jumble of bones buried under the house in Gloucester. Of their twelve victims, only one – Lucy Partington – was middle-class, well-educated, and from a close and loving family. She was missed the moment she disappeared. There was a massive nationwide hunt for her and her mother provided the police with a detailed, hour-by-hour account of her last week of normal life (she read *Wuthering Heights* by the fire, made a stew, wrapped Christmas presents, went for a walk...).

None of the other victims was remembered in this way. Many were in care or had drifted into a kind of homelessness. Some had kind of boyfriends who were kind of worried when they didn't turn up on dates, but then forgot them. Some had friends who vaguely wondered what had happened to them. The police were – in some cases – eventually informed that they seemed to have disappeared and they were put on the long missing persons list (a town the size of Bath; Britain's ghost community). But in reality these girls and young women had been missing for a long time before they were led through the gates of 25 Cromwell

Street. They belonged nowhere, in no family and no community. They'd fallen through every safety net. Their lives left little mark and we never even knew they were gone. So they dissolved back into the past, like shadows. This, for me, was the 'truth' behind the West trial. It was not just a gothic horror story of ghastly sexual torture and unimaginable individual pain – de Sade in Middle England, Hieronymous Bosch behind net curtains. Behind that was a larger tale of girls who had gone missing but had never been missed. They stood for all the people we don't care about; all the tragedies we never see; the lives we choose not to notice.

But in Soham, Jessica and Holly were missed as soon as they were gone. By nightfall the village (including its caretaker, freshly showered) was out looking for them, calling their names over the wet lanes, the empty playgrounds and the darkening fields. The police were there with their dogs. Very soon, the cameras were there too. The meaning of Soham lay outside the actual event, which was like a ghastly little rip in the British year. It lay in what we brought to that event: the media circus, the millions of words and images, the public hunger for the story, the collective grief which was both frantically sincere and yet inauthentic and shallow. Jessica and Holly were only ten and they were 'good girls', beloved by their families, popular with their friends, liked by teachers, part of a close-knit community. They had the shine of innocence on them and were pure victims, untarnished by experience. We could identify with them. They were the way little girls should be; the way we would like our own sons and daughters to be. Their mothers and fathers, decent and blameless and now tormented, were also templates of what we think of as proper parenthood.

***

We understand with words and stories, through the linked chain of events. But we recollect in pictures. Memory freeze-frames. Our lives are held in a series of vivid stills inside our head, and so it is with more public events. News is often encapsulated by a handful of photographs that select particular images from the mêlée of life. Because they are strange, beautiful, brutal; because they give us the version we want, or seem like a window into the incomprehensible, they become unforgettable. The general becomes the particular and the particular burns its way into our consciousness the way numbers and even words never can, stilled into a moment of light and shade. And in a way that was impossible for our ancestors, we look daily at pictures of the dead – those who were dead at the time, or who died thereafter. We stare into their eyes as if they could stare back from the irrevocable history: as if it were not already too late. A photograph is full of the insistence of being present, but of course it is always in the past. Much of its power lies in this insistent, melancholy duality: then and now.

The murder of Jessica Chapman and Holly Wells had both the story and it had the picture. The story was like a classic whodunnit, almost old-fashioned in its inclusion of all the required ingredients: the disappearance and search, the tight-knit village, the red herrings, the bumbling police, the outside detectives (in the shape of the media, who were both conduit and collaborator) and the handsome stranger with the careful smile who wormed his way into the community to commit such a monstrous act. It had an element of modernity to it as well: the story was led by journalists. Ian Huntley and Maxine Carr were a media-canny and celebrity-hungry pair (some journalists even called them, among themselves, during the first few days of the trial, the 'Posh and Becks of the Old Bailey', although as the evidence continued the joke died on their lips). And Ian Huntley was a paedophile with a history of sexual assault on young teenagers, and while paedophilia might not be a peculiarly twenty-first century activity, it is a twenty-first century anxiety.

And the picture – well, the picture was heart-rendingly perfect in every detail. The two friends, one blonde and one dark-haired, stand side by side in their red Manchester United shirts, with eager faces. Their eyes shine. They glow with health, happiness, life. Above them, the clock stands at four minutes past five. We know as we look at the picture that one hour later the girls will leave the house and walk down the road – giggling, arm in arm, feet in time – until they reach that road, that house, that moment, that man.

In the story, there are a series of if-onlys and so-nearlys and a futile sense of happenstance (Jessica had asked to go to the supermarket with her mother, but was discouraged; the two girls nearly didn't get together because another friend of Holly's was staying with her earlier; the walk they took together through the village that evening was a random and meandering one), creating a poignant, alternative ordinary world in which the rest of us were living that afternoon, where the murder never happened: Ian Huntley went on washing his car and no two little girls dressed in red passed by. Looking at the photo, we almost think we can stop the clock. We feel we were there with them. But of course we are only distant spectators.

It was not a meaning that we recognised and responded to, or a larger truth, but an emotion. When we talked about Soham to each other, we didn't use the language of thought but the more seductive language of feeling: gushingly sincere, sentimental, imprecise, undiscriminating, unpolitical, sorrowful and absolutely riveting. In our own way, we felt we were also, if diffusely, victims of the crime as well. We didn't keep our distance from the individual story of suffering but insisted on suffering as well, alongside those in agony. We wore ribbons, signed books of condolence, observed several minutes of silence, took flowers to their shrine. Somehow, our helpless and ostentatious sorrow made us feel as if we were doing something to help (which of course we were not) and made us feel better about ourselves.

Emotion: this is our new religion for an age without faith – a religion filled with its own rapidly evolving rites, everyday liturgies and a Medieval irrationality. Not God but the labyrinthine and endlessly fascinating inner self; not politics but a free-floating passion; not self-examination and responsibility but narcissism, blame and self-pity; not hard-won morality but an easy democracy of emotion; not neighbourhood but what a recent study by the think-tank Civitas called 'recreational grief' and 'conspicuous compassion'.

In Soham, the private became public. Victims became heroes. Suffering was transformed into a virtue. The sensational collective grief celebrated and ennobled psychological pain. A consoling therapeutic language of hurt and of healing flooded over every detail of the case. So, in our self-imposed pilgrimage of pain, we waited, we hoped, we wept at the death, we laid flowers at the shrine, we reached out to strangers. We made the country into a community of sincere yet phony mourners, the killer into a fairytale monster, and the two little girls into beloved icons and vivid, sweet-faced ghosts.

Missing

It was a very ordinary day – the kind of damp summer day most parents are thoroughly familiar with. Jessica had just got back from holiday in Menorca with her family and wanted to see her friend; she'd bought her a dolphin necklace (that would later turn up in the bin in the hangar, along with their burnt clothing: Holly's Marks & Spencer black bra, bought the day before in a rehearsal for adolescence; the Tesco and the Princess knickers; the Umbro tracksuit trousers...)

The three girls (Holly's friend from the previous night's sleep-over was there in the morning), and later the two of them, hung around the house. They chatted and giggled. They had a light lunch. They played computer games. They went out to buy some sweets. They had a thoroughly

English barbecue, cooked under shelter and eaten in the kitchen (burgers, salad, spare ribs – the contents of which were later found in their stomachs by the pathologists). At some point they changed their clothes, so that the two of them were dressed in identical Manchester United football shirts (two millimetre threads, both round and crimped; forty-nine fibre transfers).

At four minutes past five, they stood under the clock and smiled at the camera and from that moment on – although they were, as their teacher later testified, good friends but 'not inseparable' – it would be Holly-and-Jessica forever, an emblematic childhood friendship. Inseparably twinned in our minds, they represented two types of little girl ('chalk and cheese', said Maxine Carr later, smiling her lop-sided smile for the TV cameras): one blonde, one dark; one 'an angel', the other 'a tomboy'; one a cheerleader, the other a swimmer; both popular, hardworking, obedient, close to their parents, beloved.

At about 6.15, without telling Nicola and Kevin Wells, the girls left the house. It was summer and, though damp and threatening rain, there were still hours of light left; their curfew was not until 8.30. They went first to the local sports centre to buy sweets, then wandered through the familiar streets (maps, large-scale and small, graphics, red dots and purple squares). Several witnesses saw them, arms linked, happy and giggling ('Look,' said a motorist to his wife, 'two little Beckhams'). A freeze-frame CCTV in boiled-sweet colours caught them crossing the car park together. There they go, feet in time. Blurred figures moving as one, arms linked, red shirts, white trainers, a ghostly recollection of their famous picture beneath the clock, spasmodic over the lights shining on the wet roads. At 18.28 and thirty seconds, they jerk to the edge of the screen. At 18.28 and forty-one seconds, they vanish. At 18.46, Jessica's mobile phone is switched off.

We know now that by the time the girls' parents started to worry, Jessica and Holly were dead, their clothes had been cut off them and they were lying in a lonely ditch, naked and with limbs tangled. By the time the police and the village were out in force, searching, Ian Huntley had returned home, showered and changed and taken his dog Sadie for a walk. He smelt of soap and after-shave. He wanted to help the police – he was, after all, the caretaker at the village school. He was a man who was always proud of his appearance and of his job. A very presentable young man, on his way up in the world.

Nicola Wells rang up Sharon Chapman to say she didn't know where the girls were. It was worrying, but only mildly. They knew they would be back soon. Kevin Wells and his son Oliver went out on their bikes to look. The police were called. The agonising search began. Neighbours, family and friends were rung and asked if they'd seen the pair. The fathers searched, looking in all the places they thought they might have gone, asking everyone they saw for information, calling out for their daughters, shouting their names down the lanes and over fields, as darkness gradually fell. 'I kept thinking they'd be home in a minute,' said Kevin Wells. But minutes turned into hours and by dawn, they were still not found.

So began the biggest police hunt ever mounted in this country – a search that started in Soham and spread out to the neighbouring areas. Within hours, the journalists descended on the village. Sniffer dogs, satellite dishes, flashing cameras – a village and then a country transfixed by absence. Every time you turned on the television, it seemed that there was a reporter standing in the centre of Soham, telling us once more that there was nothing to say. Nothing – and yet nothing still had to be said, hour after hour and day after day. The public needed to be kept up to date with this horrible nothing. We watched the two sets of parents appeal for their daughters' return. Four collapsed faces; words hardly able to be uttered. Just come home.

Everyone knew and didn't want to know that by now they couldn't just come home. They were only ten, after all – where could two happy ten-year-olds have gone? The mothers knew exactly what their daughters were wearing on the day they disappeared; they could account for everything they'd done, minute by minute, everything they'd eaten or drunk, things they had said and plans they had had. They were vigilant parents. Jessica and Holly had been sucked out of lives that were packed with tender, matter-of-fact manifestations of love and attentiveness.

There were posters up in people's windows. One was in the window of the caretaker's house. There were meetings in the village hall – the young caretaker put out chairs. There were red herrings and surges of despair and of hope. Someone had seen the girls; a clairvoyant knew they were alive; there was freshly dug earth that turned out to be a badger's set. The caretaker had seen a strange man running across the field; he'd seen an unfamiliar red Fiesta; he spread stories about the previous caretaker who had been dismissed for inappropriate behaviour with female students.

Residents of the village were interviewed by the journalists who swarmed around Soham. What could they say, except what everyone else was saying? That they were hoping, praying. That it was a terrible thing. Two of the residents were more interviewed than the others: the caretaker Ian Huntley and his chirpy girlfriend, Maxine Carr, who had been the teaching assistant in Holly and Jessica's class that summer term. Maxine Carr had a poignant farewell card that Holly had made her at the end of term. She held it up so that viewers could read it clearly. She wore a shirt that said 'Scored!' on it; a pale face, a lopsided smile and a tumble of reddish-brown hair. She and Huntley became a familiar couple on our television screens, minor celebrities who frowned and looked appropriately sad and sometimes even had tears in their eyes, and became more fluent the more they were interviewed.

It emerged that Huntley was the last person to have seen the the girls. They'd walked past his door when he was outside washing the dog, and stopped to ask him about 'Miss Carr'. He said, to anyone who asked, that he had told them that Miss Carr wasn't very happy because she had failed to get the permanent job she had applied for at their school. But – unfortunately, he said – Maxine wasn't around to talk to them because she was in the bath.

Ian Huntley, on television, had an endearing, heavy-browed shyness about him, an anxiety and hesitancy that struck the right note. By the Thursday after the girls' disappearance, he had found his script and was refining it. He reiterated that Jessica and Holly seemed happy, giggly. He wished, in hindsight, that he'd found out more where they had been going. He talks about Holly's father, 'Kev' (this dreadful intimacy continued even in court). He used the familiar jargon of feeling: 'I pray they're alive and well'; 'It's just dreadful'; 'Get on the phone and just come home'; 'There's always a glimmer of hope'. He says: 'It's very upsetting to think that I might have been the last friendly face the girls had to speak to.' In court his media-savvy composure was used against him, yet I think he was sincere (though of course not authentic). He believed himself and was moved by his own words.

Maxine Carr was more glib and self-confident than her boyfriend (after all, she had so much less to hide and to fear). She was a TV natural, a wonderfully good liar, enjoying her few days of fame. She chimes in to agree with Huntley's version of events that night, improvising a few vivid details. She talks of the girls with affection: they're 'brilliant kids... Holly like a doll, very girly, very bright... Jess, she loved her sport, a tomboy type... like chalk and cheese...'

She puts herself gaily in the centre of the story, telling reporters how they wanted to be her bridesmaids when she married, how they wanted her back in school and, when she didn't get the permanent post, kept looking at her with tears in their eyes, how she loved children. For both these two, the true story slid away, and they were acting out a fantasy version of their lives, in which they were two attractive young people, responsible and kind, in love with each other and eager to help.

A week later, their story – already under considerable suspicion, both from police and also journalists who in this case were sleuths as well as reporters – fell apart. The bodies of Jessica Chapman and Holly Wells were discovered, naked and decomposing in a ditch in Lakenheath, forty-five minutes' drive from Soham. Their half-burnt clothes were found in the hangar of the school where Huntley was caretaker, and for which he had the keys.

It is a maxim of forensic science that a criminal always leaves something at the scene of crime and always takes something away: the fibres from their famous red shirts were on his clothes; the fibres from his clothes were on their shirts; mud from the rutted country lane was on the sill of his car. Ian Huntley and Maxine Carr were arrested. A ripple of gleeful horror ran through the country. Two of them! People talked about the Wests, about Brady and Hindley.

Two minutes of silence was observed all over the country, in shops and on high streets, in sports meetings and in homes. Two minutes, as if the traditional one minute was no longer sufficient to contain the nation's grief. Flowers piled high in the sombre village. David Beckham – who earlier had appealed for the girls release and whose name was on the back of their red football shirts – dedicated his first goal of the season to the murdered children. John Howard, president of Australia, dispatched roses on behalf of his country. Prince Charles sent handwritten letters to the parents of the girls. The public queued to sign the book of condolences in St Andrew's Church and many thousands more signed the virtual book of condolences on the internet.

There was a 'Soham rose' created in their honour. There were trauma counsellors dispatched to help the family and friends, but also to help people who, though strangers, felt they too had suffered some psychological crisis. CCTV cameras were erected on the streets where the girls had meandered on their last walk ('You won't see ten-year-old children without their parents now,' said one Soham resident to a reporter).

Before long, there were what Patrick West calls in his *Conspicuous Compassion*, grief tourists, who visited Soham in cars and coaches as a site of special interest. They went to the church and stared at the college and made the pilgrimage that retraced Jessica and Holly's last journey. An ordinary, slightly run-down town in Cambridgeshire, where nothing much happened, was infused with a quasi-religious importance.

As the girls were sanctified, so Huntley and Carr were reviled, even before the evidence against them was made public. The crowds that were quick to weep were also quick to hate and blame. Buying flowers turned to throwing eggs and stones at the sides of prison vans; adoration became vindictiveness. Maxine Carr – who, it would emerge, was a marginal figure, not wicked but childish and stupid – was called Myra Hindley mark two. Hell was too good for Ian Huntley. Crowds turned up at Peterborough Magistrates court to boo and hold up placards. A Soham resident told me that the punishment he would like to see meted out, once the pair was found guilty, was for them to be set down in the centre of Soham and left there. 'That would be justice.'

The media continued to feed the public appetite for the story with tantalising nuggets: a reporter sneaked into the prison where Huntley was held, under the guise of being a warder; Huntley's love letters to Maxine Carr were leaked to the press; Carr had broken off with him; he had tried to kill himself; she had tried to kill herself.

In the meantime, as the trial approached, was postponed, and then fixed for November of 2003, journalists were digging up background. They wanted to be ready for the guilty verdict, when hundreds of thousands of words would give us the 'whole story', the 'exclusive story', the 'true story', of how a psychopath had been created and gone among us and no one had recognised him, of how 'evil' lurks in the most ordinary places, of how no one is safe any more. We wanted to know what happened, and why, and what it all meant. That's what the trial at Court Number One in the Old Bailey was meant to give us.

The Caretaker's Trial

In court, real life and art meet. A trial is like a play, structured and gripping. It's like a philosophical debate, in which facts may be accepted but interpretations conflict. It's also about people's lives and their deaths, people's crimes and their excuses. The trial of Ian Huntley and Maxine Carr, which began with painstaking slowness and built up to an extraordinary psychological climax, was riveting drama. But when the curtain fell on the final act, and the main players withdrew from the stage, there was a verdict but not the satisfaction of a final answer. We will never know the full truth of what happened in 5 College Close. There is only one person who can tell us and it seems improbable that he ever will. Locked up alone with himself, the cells around him empty, he is silent. He claims he cannot remember the moment of the deaths, as if his mind became like a psychological version of the heart of the crime: a black hole, a terrifying void.

On the twentieth day of the Soham trial at the Old Bailey, Ian Huntley walked from the glass-sided dock into the witness box, took the oath, and in a low, scarcely audible voice began to tell his version of the deaths of ten-year-old Jessica Chapman and Holly Wells. For two and a half days he went over and over his story in all its grim detail, while at the back of the court the parents of the girls sat and listened, as they had listened day after day and week after week. He was the only witness in his own defence, and the only person who knows the full truth about what happened on that wet summer evening in August. With him, after sixteen months of waiting, we arrived at last at the heart of the case; at the threshold of its mystery.

In the previous four weeks of the trial, the prosecution had presented its case against Ian Huntley and Maxine Carr. They gave a meticulously detailed account of the events that led up to the girls' disappearance, and then away from it; the innocent before and the nightmarish after; the last known seconds of the girls' meandering progress through familiar streets, arms linked; and then the frantic, increasingly heart-rending search that came to an end when the bodies were found.

But right at the start of the trial, the counsel for the prosecution, Richard Latham, had unexpectedly revealed in his opening speech that Huntley would concede that he had let the girls into his home, that he was the only one present at their deaths, and that he had dumped their bodies. Nevertheless, though pleading guilty to perverting the course of justice, he was pleading not guilty to the charges of murder. And on Tuesday November 25, in the final few minutes of the day when Stephen Coward QC, Huntley's lawyer, was cross-examining the Home Office pathologist Dr Nathaniel Cary, there was another dramatic revelation: Holly Wells had died when Ian Huntley had accidentally knocked her into a bath, said Coward. Jessica died when Ian Huntley put a hand across her mouth to stop her from screaming.

All of the rest of the evidence – the minute-by-minute reconstructions of the girls' movements and of Huntley's, the forensic examination of fibres (there were 154 transfers of fibres), pollen, tyre tracks, fingerprints, mud, blood – had circled around this black hole at the centre: what happened inside 5 College Close, between 18.31, when the girls were last seen by the CCTC camera and 18.46, when Jessica's phone was switched off? And behind this question, of course, lurked another question: why did it happen? Why did Jessica and Holly die that evening?

In June 2003, after Maxine Carr had broken all contact with him, Ian Huntley tried to kill himself in prison, taking a near-fatal overdose that sent him into a coma. Afterwards, he claimed that he started to recover the buried memories of that terrible evening, and he made a promise to his parents that he would come to the court to tell the truth so that the girls' parents would at last know what happened to their little daughters.

His story, which he was carefully led through by his lawyer, was that he was outside his house cleaning Sadie, the mucky dog, when the girls came down the road; that he took Holly and Jessica into his house because Holly had a nosebleed; took them upstairs into the bathroom where Holly sat on the edge of the full bath and he gave her tissues to staunch it; took Holly into his bedroom, to sit on the bed while Jessica used the toilet; took Holly back into the bathroom where she could finish cleaning up her nosebleed; accidentally knocked Holly into the full bath and heard a splash; froze in panic; placed his hand over Jessica's mouth because she was screaming, 'You pushed her.'

Huntley said that he never meant either death to happen ('One died as a result of my inability to act and the other died as a direct result of my actions', was how he put it on the following day, under cross-examination) and that after-

33

wards, when he had pulled Holly from the bath and checked her pulse which was still, and leant his cheek to Jessica's mouth and felt for breath that wasn't there, he vomited in the hallway outside the bathroom, and then sat huddled, semi-conscious, in the corner. His story, of course, was absurdly implausible, though he may have believed it himself. Perhaps he believes it still. The mind has complicated mechanisms to protect itself from itself.

His story didn't end there. He took Jessica's mobile out of her pocket and switched it off; he carried their bodies down the stairs and after checking no one was around, bundled them into the cramped boot of his car, bending their legs to fit them in; he collected petrol and bin bags (to protect his feet and thus conceal evidence), he drove to Lakenheath and found a lonely track; he got out where the vegetation grew thickly and he rolled the two girls down into the ditch; he climbed into the ditch and cut off their clothing which he would later partially burn back in Soham – their red football shirts and their tracksuit trousers, their knickers, Holly's black bra which she and her mother had bought the day before – and then he poured petrol ('backwards and forwards' and 'left to right') over their bodies and threw on a match. The flames flared and he climbed back into the car, turned around, and drove away.

And the story didn't end there either, of course. It left that lonely track and rejoined the route we are all familiar with by now: the eleven days of careful concealment, of repeated interviews given to police and journalists in which he spoke about how the girls came to the door of his house ('giggly', 'happy') and then walked away again; eleven days of lying and misdirection and even of approaching Holly's father ('Kev') to express sympathy – until, in the early hours of August 17th, he was arrested and plunged into a silence that lasted until September 2003, when he finally told his legal team that the girls had died in his house; that he had been with them when they died; that he had disposed of their bodies.

Stories get picked apart under cross-examination. Single words are scrutinised; phrases deconstructed. Tiny inconsistencies are gazed at until they magnify. Narrative is broken into separate pieces: the threshold, the bathroom, the bedroom, the bodies, the conspiracy and cover-up.

Ian Huntley was actually inside the house, suggested Richard Latham QC, when the girls came down the road; Maxine Carr's statement had placed him there, with the television on, and the dog un-dirty after all. So it wasn't by chance that he met the girls at the door, he was 'watching'. 'No,' said Huntley. He was 'annoyed' after a phone call with Maxine Carr, in which she'd told him she was going out 'again' with her mother that evening in Grimsby ('Do you like to control people?' asked Richard Latham. 'She was out of your control. Did that irritate you?) and just minutes later, when he saw Jessica and Holly, 'it was just too tempting, wasn't it... two girls of ten?'

'If you mean what I think you mean, no,' said Huntley. 'You lured them into the house, didn't you?' 'I did not', said Huntley. And he used the pretence that Maxine Carr was in the house to make them feel safe. They knew Maxine was away, said Huntley.

The possibility of a sexual motive behind the deaths of Holly and Jessica dominated many of the exchanges in the trial – first between Huntley and the prosecution and again, later, when Maxine Carr took the stand. Huntley admitted to taking Holly into the bedroom (he agreed this was 'inappropriate'). He said she sat upon the bed, and a single drop of blood fell on the sheets, for which she apologised – later Maxine Carr would insist that on her return from Grimsby the entire duvet and its cover was cleaned and wet in the washing-machine, although Ian Huntley was a 'slob' who slouched on the couch, never washed up, left crumbs everywhere, never used the vacuum cleaner.

Time after time, Huntley was forced back to the actual deaths. First Holly: 'And you watched her drown.' 'I just froze.' 'You watched her drown.' 'I wasn't watching.'

'Holly drowned in that bath because you wanted her dead.'
'I did not want her dead.' 'The only way that child would
have drowned in the bath is if you were holding her under
the water.' 'I was not holding her...'

And of Jessica, whose smothering he was made to
demonstrate by placing his hand over his own mouth:
'Something prevented her from turning her head. Once
again, please – what were you doing with your other hand?'
'I don't know.' 'What must you have been doing with your
other hand?' 'Probably restraining her somehow.' 'This was
a fit, active ten-year old who... would have been doing
what?' 'Struggling.' 'Fighting for her very life.' 'Yes.' '...If
you had given that girl the slightest chance, she would have
lived.' 'Yes.' 'You didn't give her the slightest chance, did
you?' 'No.'

He was also forced to describe how it felt to deal with
the bodies of the girls; the horror of the questions drove
him into silence. 'Which did you pick up first?... What did
it feel like, this girl's body, when you did that?' 'Limp.'
'Difficult to carry, no?' 'Yes.' 'Because a dead body is
floppy?' 'Yes.' 'Her body was wet, wasn't it?' 'Yes.' 'How
did it feel as you carried this dead body down the stairs, Mr
Huntley?' No answer. 'How did it feel?' No answer again.
'How did it feel when you carried Jessica's body down the
stairs? That you had just killed?' Another long pause.

'Well?' 'Not good,' said Huntley.

At one point during his day of insistent probing, Huntley lost his temper: When Richard Latham asked him to explain his actions after Holly fell into the bath, he raised his voice: 'In these circumstances, you can be very rational. In those circumstances, it is not so rational.' Then he snapped, 'Believe me, I know.' 'You can get quite angry, can't you Mr Huntley?' said the prosecution lawyer in reply. 'Yes.' 'You just lost your temper with me, didn't you?'

***

Guilty of the murder of Jessica Chapman, said the jury. Guilty of the murder of Holly Wells. Life, said the judge; life for the man who took life and who showed 'no mercy and no regret'; whose only tears were shed for himself.

And so Ian Huntley, who for years had stalked the young and vulnerable, and who for six wretched weeks, for sixteen months, had stalked our imaginations, was walked from the dock, face expressionless, and vanished from public view. Gradually, he will become just a ghostly name among all those other names that, when we think of them, send a little shiver down the spine. Remember him? In the dock, he looked a bit like a tense-shouldered Russell

Crowe, but with doughy, prison-pallid skin; duller eyes. He once had a slender girlfriend with a mop of hair and a nearly pretty face. He once was the caretaker – the paedophile, the predator, the rapist, the murderer: the man who had for years been molesting and raping girls and young women, and who had fallen through all the cracks in the criminal justice system. The man who one wet evening in August 2002 killed two ten-year-old girls. The curtain fell on the long, heartbreaking drama.

We now know too much, defiled by details, yet still we don't know. At the inky heart of the case, in that little hole in time, the silence remained.

Many of the murder cases that have gripped the nation in recent years possess the horror of the strange; the spooky dread of the unknown. Two ten-year-old boys snatch a toddler from outside a shop, walk him to a railway line and kill him there; a 'good' doctor gives lethal injections to dozens, hundreds, of his patients and it's impossible to comprehend the mind that took pleasure in these blank and bureaucratic crimes; a couple sexually torture lost and unmourned young women and their own children, then murder them and bury them vertically under the floor of their terraced slaughter house; a little girl, running home across fields, is snatched by a stranger in a van, like a nasty modern fairytale (many of us probably don't even recall Roy Whiting's name – rather than being an individual for us, he became the wicked wolf, the fictive bogeyman). Ian Huntley exploded into view, in a violent transformation from apparently sensible and steady young man to brutal killer. That he was dangerous and sick we now all know, a bomb waiting to explode. On August 4th, random events combined and lit the fuse. A predator, not a loner; a moment, not a plan.

In this case we have been gripped as well by the familiar, and that is why we care so much about them (and often so little about other murders). In the summer of last year, when Jessica and Holly first went missing, it was – to borrow one of the clichés that filled the newspapers – 'every parent's nightmare'. They lived in the kind of village where, as residents said, 'these things just don't happen'; they went to the local school. They were close to their parents, loyal to their friends (and one of them must have watched the other being killed). They seemed like a template for a proper, decent, safe and well-protected childhood – the way young girls, on the brink of adolescence but not yet there, should be; the way we'd like our own children to be. It was this sentimental identification that filled the media, prompted the national outpouring of grief, and seemed to be trying to flood the great gap between those who knew the girls, and the strangers who spuriously felt they knew them. Yet, as Justice Moses sternly said, what the parents must feel cannot be imagined and cannot be shared. There is no emotional equivalent. They are alone with their grief and we cannot join them.

**

Ian Huntley and Maxine Carr became linked and demonised in the public imagination but she was a hundred miles away, in Grimsby, when the girls died. He acted alone, and she was on the margin of the story. In the court they sat in the glass-sided dock and never looked at each other, not even when he edged past her on his way to the witness box. She was tipped slightly away from him, her head slewed to the side and sometimes leaning forward so her hair hid her face. He stared ahead. His expression never wavered, although once or twice he looked downwards, fiddled with a button on his jacket, tightened his knuckles.

'Psychopath', some journalists said during the proceedings. 'Look at that brow.' How can you ever tell from a face what lies behind? The parents of Jessica and Holly also sat in court, day after day and week after week, and they maintained a dignified demeanour even when Ian Huntley was telling the jury how he crammed the girls' bodies into the boot of his car. If there are lessons from this trial, one must be how much is concealed under the implacable surface and how hidden most people are from each other. Paedophiles don't always look like the seventy-three-year-old Arnold Hartley who was battered to death in his house in November of 2003, as the trial of Huntley was going on, who had a stubbly, jowly face and an eye patch, like a down-at-heel bandit on a peeling 'Wanted' poster. They look like Ian Huntley too (but 'I know him,' cried Maxine Carr when she heard from the police that the man she had hoped to marry was charged with the murder); they look like us. This was one of the dreads of the case: that we keep so much of our strangeness and our turmoil secret, each of us unknowing and unknown. That you cannot protect your children, because kindness and great cruelty often wear the same face.

The motif of clearing up and of cleaning away – Maxine was the spring-cleaner of all time, wielding her Flash, her bleach, her Mr Sheen and Shake 'n' Vac, washing those curtains, scraping at the tiles until the paint flaked, polishing the underside of the table, desperately trying to erase the nasty stains of life – had as its shadow version the motif of dirt and ghastly disorder. Ian Huntley, narcissistically clean in person, was a domestic slob and a couch potato; he lay on his sofa, drinking lager and scattering crumbs. He left dishes in the sink, laundry in a heap. And then, in a nightmarish psychological version of squalour, he broke the bath, flooded the dining-room, killed two little girls, vomited on the carpet, dragged their bodies through his house and into his car. Inner and outer worlds had all of a sudden collided like mucky breakers crashing over the sea walls.

In the story the trial told, conflicting versions jostled. The blizzard of details the prosecution produced were meticulous and almost irrelevant, because we knew, right from the start, that the two girls had died in Ian Huntley's house, and he had dumped their bodies. In a sense the evidence provided the bricks and mortar of the case; Huntley had threaded his thin and frantic line of defence around their incontestability. Never mind the laminated maps, mobile-phone beacons, car tracks on the lonely lane in Lakenheath, fingerprints on the black bin bag; never mind the solid edifice of clues and circumstances – what dominated the trial was the black hole at its centre. It is still there.

What always mattered was the tale that Huntley would tell and then how the prosecution would make him un-tell it, undoing the story, turning words back on themselves, looking at the slippages through which truth might seep. The Huntley we had glimpsed during other witnesses' brief statements was a fragile, weakly defended man, with few inner resources. He could be a bully (self-righteously eject-ing journalists from the school where they were writing their articles), but was thin-skinned too. He stood stolidly enough in the dock, but in life he lost his temper, cried easily – cried in front of the Vice-Principal of the school where he worked; cried in front of the police when they came to ask questions. Maxine Carr, in her garrulous original statements to the police after she was charged, insisted that her boyfriend, even if he had killed the girls, would have broken down at once. He was an anxious, even depressive person (anxiety is one of the dominant impres-sions of him in photographs – tense, with a tight, vigilant smile), and had a prickly sense of his status – he was quick to insist that he was not a caretaker but a site-manager, or even a 'senior site-manager'.

What grabs you are the details – those sinister fissures through which the 'real' Ian Huntley could be seen. When he was being led through his story by Stephen Coward, QC, he was calm and articulate. If you set aside the absurdity of an account in which the two fit and active girls both died accidentally in two different ways in a matter of seconds because he panicked, the strangest aspect was his repeated use of the present tense when he talked about his life in Soham, with Maxine – 'We do this... we do that... we have a television in the kitchen.' And he eerily repeated this under cross-examination, as if his domestic routine and his relationship was still going on and soon enough he would walk back into it in his Chinos and his trainers, hair stiff and straight, and be senior site-manager, couch potato and Maxine's boyfriend once again. (Later, during her testimony, Maxine Carr shoved Ian Huntley firmly into the past tense and while he called her 'Maxine', she referred to him as 'Mr Huntley', 'that man', and once, flinging out her hand towards the dock where he stood, even 'that thing'.)

But under cross-examination the story cracked open and so, every so often, did he. Smooth talk stalled into silence, into 'I don't know', 'I can't recall'. The dog-ate-my-homework excuse for the two deaths became a series of admissions: 'I killed Jessica...' 'She would have struggled...' 'It was inexcusable...' He lost his temper once, when pressed on the irrationality of his lie, and at times he seemed genuinely aggrieved with the prosecution, as if part of him believed his own unbelievable story. 'You've already made up your mind,' he snapped, bitterly. Self-pity has been one of the motifs of this trial; a narcissism that leaves no room for the sufferings of others. Pity – pity for the girls whose lives were blotted out; pity for the parents and family who sat day after day listening to this bleakest tale – was absent. Yet, he said, with a sanctimoniousness worthy of Uriah Heep, he had promised his mother he would make it through to this trial so that he could tell the truth to the parents about their daughters' deaths.

It seems plausible that Huntley's version of that Sunday evening was a relic of the truth he would not tell – the dog was probably dirty, Holly probably had a nosebleed, the girls wanted to know how 'Miss Carr' was, in some way or other he panicked, he didn't set out to commit murder but, having killed one he had to do away with the other, he vomited on the carpet outside the bathroom. Maybe he actually did black out, as he claimed. A reported forty per cent of homicides cannot remember the moment of murder. The body revolts; the mind shuts down in horror at itself. 'I do not know' means 'I will not know'; 'I cannot recall' means 'I must not remember'.

Bit by bit, from Huntley's inadequate version, another story emerged, one which could never be wholly spoken aloud during the trial but which lurked in the margins and between the lines. The great why? Why did they die?

Paedophiles, says Cleo van Velsen, a consultant psychiatrist in forensic psychotherapy who works in a secure unit, are most usually age-specific, but Huntley's sexuality had unravelled into an undiscriminating compulsion to humiliate and control. Since 1995, he had been accused of nine sexual offences, including a string of rapes, an indecent assault of an eleven-year-old girl, and unlawful sexual intercourse with four young girls. There were certainly more unreported cases, possibly many more. As soon as he was convicted, the anecdotes and personal testimonies streamed out, so that reading the papers the following day felt pornographically squalid and terrifying – he was a serial rapist, a despoiler of the young and vulnerable, he was consistently violent, controlling and abusive, he kept one girlfriend prisoner, he kicked a girlfriend in the stomach so she miscarried, he half-strangled another, he hit another down the stairs... The pattern gives clear evidence of a brutalising sexuality.

And then, on that August evening, he had an argument on the phone with Maxine about her going out that evening (she could, he said, get a bit 'flirty' when she had too much to drink – and photographs published in the tabloids after the verdict show him to be right there, for she did go out on the razzle that particular night) and she sent him a curt text message at 18.31. Seconds later, Jessica Chapman and Holly Wells came down the road. Somehow he lured them into his house – by saying Maxine Carr was there? He took them upstairs. At 18.46, if we are to follow the evidence of Jessica's mobile being turned off then, they were dead. We do not know what happened in those thirteen or fourteen minutes. We know that they were in the bathroom, in the bedroom. We know that he cut their clothes off their bodies, removed their underwear, tried to wash the duvet and its cover.

When he was preparing to dump the girls' bodies – collecting bin bags, rubber gloves, the petrol can to douse them and set them alight – Huntley also changed out of his smart 'Brushers' and into his trainers. Why? Because, he explained, as if there was nothing odd about personal vanity in the middle of brutal double murder , he only wore his Brushers in the house; he didn't want to get them messy. When, during the subsequent days of lying, he approached Kevin Wells, it was to say to him that he was very sorry, he hadn't known it 'was your daughter'. Under cross-examination, he denied that this was playing with the emotions of the father. He had been speaking the truth: he hadn't known and he was sorry. This was mocked by Latham and used as evidence of his ruthlessness, used again in the judge's impassioned closing speech, but it had the weird ring of of truth.

Ian Huntley was, in this own way, apologising. 'Kev', he called him then. 'Kev' he called him again in court: Kev to the man whose daughter he'd killed. This is a psychopathic apology, emptied of sorrow and replaced instead with self – the same self that he paraded in his television interviews, talking of the glimmer of hope and talking of being the last 'friendly face'; the same self that felt misunderstood by the prosecuting counsel, that changed out of his smart boots so as not to dirty them when dumping the little girls.

Is Ian Huntley a psychopath then? We quickly rush to such labels, for our culture is fascinated by murders committed by emotionally perverted individuals who are driven by hidden inner compulsions. Crime is seen as the inevitable outcome of pathology – and then we can call some individuals evil and have done with it. It's so easy. Evil psychopath; bring back capital punishment – the mourning crowd who laid flowers for the dead can quickly become a lynch mob.

The Hare Psychopathy checklist (developed by Robert Hare, and originating in a book by Hervey Cleckley called *The Mask of Sanity*) has among the traits listed: glibness and superficial charm, a grandiose sense of self-worth, pathological lying, need for stimulation and proneness to boredom, cunning and manipulation, lack of remorse or guilt, lack of empathy, short-term relationships, criminal versatility – and at first glance Huntley seems to fit almost too neatly into the category. Cleo van Velsen agrees his behaviour falls into psychopathy – particularly his ability to compartmentalise. 'Not to be connected with what you're doing,' she says. 'Not to be overwhelmed by horror or guilt.' Psychopaths, she says, have a real capacity to seem sane and normal.

***

There are specific and important lessons to be learnt from the case, but most of these are managerial, bureaucratic ones to do with rules and procedures. There were grave errors made by the police before and after the murder of Holly Wells and Jessica Chapman – in fact, two chief constables made secret visits to the girls' parents to confess to the blunders that had allowed Huntley to slip through the net. Huntley was given his job as caretaker although he had been accused of a series of sex crimes in Humberside, before he moved to Soham. The vetting procedure did not even pick up that he had been taken to court accused of raping an eighteen-year-old girl. It also missed three other rape allegations against him, three complaints of under-age sex with girls between the ages of thirteen and fifteen, and one of indecently assaulting a girl of eleven. Huntley had applied for the job under his mother's maiden name, Nixon, but also included the name Huntley on the police check form, yet only the name Nixon was checked on the police national computer, and it yielded no results. Due to the failings of the system elsewhere, the name Huntley

50

wouldn't have yielded any results either.

Immediately after the girls' disappearance, Humberside police told their Cambridgeshire colleagues they had no information on Huntley. Cambridgeshire forces, snowed under with the responses from the public, ignored phone calls from those in Grimsby claiming to recognise Huntley from television pictures who had information about him. It was the journalists who suspected Huntley from the start. Kevin and Nicola Wells were always concerned about the police investigation – they claim they were left to learn of leads from the media, and had struggled during the investigation's first forty-eight hours to persuade the police to treat Holly as a possible victim of crime.

'They were looking for a stranded child or a runaway,' said Kevin Wells. 'We told them there had been no family arguments. We tried to impress on them our dread, because parents just know their child, but we just couldn't persuade them there had been no row or trauma and this was not Holly's idea of a prank.'

He said that, as the frantic hunt went on, he carried an image in his head of 'Holly bound, perhaps gagged, tied to a chair in someone's front room, and I thought I might catch a glimpse of her through a chink in the curtains and I could smash my way in, take her in my arms and tell her it was OK because Daddy had come.' In fact she was dead long before they realized she was missing. The police blunders only prolonged the agony of waiting and delayed suspicion falling on Huntley.

**

Apart from the gaping flaws in the system, which allowed a man with a crowded history of violent sexual offences to end up as a school caretaker, what other lessons are to be learned? How is a psychopath, a paedophile created? How did Ian Huntley turn into the young man who bullied, raped, abused, and finally murdered? Everything is simple in hindsight. We look at Huntley's life and can see how he grew up crookedly, and recognise the signs of a murder that was bound to happen, as if the clock was always ticking forward to this moment and this time. We can track back to see how we got here. But can we do it the other way round? Can we find the men who are going to turn into Ian Huntley or Ian Brady or Peter Sutcliffe?

Ian Kevin Huntley was born in 1974, in Immingham, an industrial port for giant container ships just north of Grimsby – a place on the margin of things, surrounded by cranes, refineries, Portakabins, industrial estates, truck services, transport warehouse, grit-blasting, hauliers. Everything is temporary, on its way somewhere else. The ships bring containers to the port and the lorries take them to the North, to the Midlands, to London, somewhere else. Everything looks away from the drab town centre.

Huntley's father, a gas-fitter, often took Ian and his younger brother Wayne to the docks, though Huntley's real passion was for planes, especially military aircraft. Twenty years later, there would be a large, framed picture of a jet fighter in the living room of his house in 5 College Close, and Lakenheath, where the girls' bodies were dumped, was his favourite plane-spotting site. He was a quiet boy, whose dream was to be a pilot in the RAF. Photographs show him smiling, wide-faced, pleasant-looking, at first with curly hair, and then, after he was bullied because of it, his now familiar cropped and flattened cut.

He had a loving mother, Lynda (although after the verdict she told a tabloid that he deserved hanging), a proud father (who says he is there for him always, in spite of what he did), a brother he adored. After primary school, he spent two unhappy years at one school where he was badly bullied, then moved to a different comprehensive. Here he was still bullied – as much verbally as physically. He was called 'Jackanory' because of the grandiose stories he told about himself, and 'Spadehead' and the 'White Cliff of Dover' because of his large forehead. Classmates remember him as a loner, the last to be picked for teams; a cocky yet insecure boy who picked fights and then ran away from them; who cried easily (a trait which survived – Margaret Bryden, deputy at Soham College, described at the trial how his eyes would fill with tears when she criticised his work). Unhappy, in other words – but with the kind of unhappiness many children feel when they don't fit in, and with the kind of defences many children use to protect themselves against the ignorant cruelty of their peers. Lots of children are bullied and are bullies, have complicated family relationships, come from broken homes, are wretched, are abandoned, feel unloved. Yet this child became the man who molested, raped, killed, and yet wore a charming face.

When he was thirteen years old, Huntley found his father Kevin in bed with a sixteen-year-old baby-sitter. Until that moment, the family had been close, but now Kevin lashed out, viciously beating his son and making him promise never to tell what he had seen. This – so the rather-too-neat story goes – was the watershed moment, when his life of lies began and his ordinary wretchedness became something altogether more disturbing and sinister. He became a bully himself. His fantasies became more powerful. Eventually, he told his mother what he had witnessed. Devastated, she moved out of the family home with her two sons and although she returned a few weeks later, the marriage was now deeply strained. Kevin began drinking heavily and was increasingly violent. His rage was almost always directed against the oldest son who had betrayed him. There would be months when they would not even speak. Yet this is the father who now says that, alone in all the world, he will stand by his son and care for him through the long years ahead.

He was bright enough to have stayed at school after GCSEs, but instead he left and began a string of menial jobs. He worked in a canning plant, assembled toilets, filleted fish, and between these had long bouts of unemployment. His life was, bit by bit, breaking down. His parents were estranged and, when his father finally moved out for good, his beloved mother began a long lesbian relationship with a young woman the same age as Huntley, called Julie Beasley. From this point his psychological instability became evident. His work attendance was erratic, there were rumours of suicide attempts – slashing his wrists or taking pills. His tall tales (that he was a pilot, a body builder, had a five-point plan to becoming a millionaire...) were mocked among his workmates, who treated him with open contempt ('that horrible little man').

At eighteen he took a serious overdose, telling doctors later it had been because of the state of his parents' marriage. He tried twice more, in 1994. He was a young man in clear need of help and not receiving it.

His escape from the misery and drudgery of his life came from chatting up girls in the pubs and clubs around Grimsby. Perhaps with them he could at last be the 'man' that he so badly wanted to be; they looked up to him and were charmed by him; admired him, and let him feel himself 'someone' at last. With young and credulous girls he could tell his stories and be believed, and could have power and control over them – control seems to have been at least as important as sex to him.

Just a few months after his suicide attempt, he met seventeen-year-old Claire Evans and, after a whirlwind romance, the couple married in January 1995, without even telling her family about it until after the ceremony. Begun quickly, ended quickly: the marriage broke down within a few days. Huntley's younger brother Wayne went to comfort Claire and an affair began. Huntley was humiliated and devastated when his brother confessed to him a month later. The two of them didn't speak for a year. Huntley resorted to lies to make himself more of a hero in the story (he told people he had discovered Wayne in bed with Claire and beaten him so badly he had ended up in hospital).

By now, Huntley's father had moved in with another woman (Sandra Brewer); his mother was living with Julie

Beasley. It was five months after the collapse of Huntley's brief marriage that he came first to the attention of the police. The parents of a fifteen-year-old girl had contacted social services, saying their daughter was involved with a twenty-one-year-old man. Their charge was to be repeated over the next few years by other anxious parents.

Huntley preyed on young girls to restore his pride and self-esteem. He was charming and a bully; he flattered and abused them. He had sex with them and beat them up. By the time he was twenty-one he had slept with at least a dozen under-age girls; some of them were fourteen or fifteen, but some were as young as eleven. He often picked them up at the pub where he played pool almost every night, or at the Friday evening disco. Sometimes the girls would arrive at his flat in their school uniform.

The girls who told their stories after Huntley was arrested for the Soham murders speak of his violent temper and the physical abuse to which they were subjected – locking them in the bedroom, kicking them, pushing them down the stairs, hitting them repeatedly. He had to have his things just so, he needed to have his dinner on the table exactly on time, he hated using condoms and refused to do so. They also described him as being more than usually vain about his appearance, repeatedly and anxiously checking himself in the mirror ('He loved himself', said one of the girls). In the next few years, nine complaints concerning sexual offences were made against him. He was becoming progressively more violent: soon the charges were of rape (between the spring of 1998 and the summer of 1999 he was accused of rape four times). Eventually he was charged with raping a woman in a dimly lit through way known as Gas Alley, but the case collapsed.

By the late 1990s, he was known in Grimsby as a paedophile. His flat was attacked, his windows smashed, his door broken down. This did nothing to stop his ugly behaviour, which by then he probably had little control over. He was frantically insecure, intensely narcissistic, chockfull of self-pity and rage. This was the man hired as caretaker at Soham College and trusted with children.

***

Yet as his own behaviour was spiralling downwards, towards the moment when he would kill two ten-year-olds, his life was upwardly mobile and seemingly going the way he wanted. He had got the £15,741-a-year job, and a newly-renovated house to go with it. He also had a steady girlfriend. He had met Maxine Carr at a Grimsby night-club in 1999. When he was invited for an interview at Soham, he asked her to go with him. She was presentable and eager and also wanted to work with children. He made a good impression at his interview: so sensible and trustworthy; such a relief to find a young man of his sort. At last people liked and accepted him – gone were the days of being 'Spadehead'; now the kids thought he was 'cool' (or, as one mother put it, 'quite hip-hop'). He was even trusted enough to supervise pupils in detention.

Fred West had a childhood of such squalor, neglect and extreme sexual depravity stretching back generations, like an animal rutting among animals, that it seemed almost inevitable that he should turn into the cunning beast who made instruments of sexual torture to use on his children and on the young people who fled to his house for help. Rosemary West was abused herself, before turning into an abuser. In court, she refused to accept any responsibility for what had happened but in prison, after many sessions of therapy, she has finally admitted to her sexually brutal behaviour and has decided not to apply for parole. Mary Bell was used as a tool in her adored mother's prostitution.

But what about Ian Huntley? His bad childhood was horribly like many bad childhoods – and indeed, his sexual behaviour was at first uncomfortably like many young men's sexual behaviour: full of promiscuity, cruelty, insecure bravado, a need to control. Even the fact that his victims were under-age looks at first quite normal, especially in a culture where youth is celebrated, and where girls are encouraged to look like women while women are encouraged to look like girls. A fifteen-year-old when he was eighteen? That might be illegal in Britain, but else-where in Europe it's not, and it's certainly not rare. But then with a fourteen-year-old, a thirteen-year-old, an eleven-year-old? Sliding down into paedophilia and dan-gerous violence. Sliding faster and faster towards that evening in August, when, after a nasty little spat with Maxine Carr on the telephone, two ten-year-olds walked past his door dressed in identical Manchester United shirts: the tomboy and the angel. So lives turn on an instant; so lives end.

He has shown no pity, nor has he admitted guilt; perhaps he doesn't feel it. Very few convicted killers take responsibility for what they have done: prisons are full to the gunnels with people who claim they are innocent. (Rosemary West's example is a rare exception.) Huntley said it was an accident – and probably in his terms it was. Humans are infinitely good at blaming others and express-ing their own emotional hurt (in the dock, Huntley was good at it too, allowing his testimony to become charged with bitterness, the sense of being misunderstood) and very bad at confessing guilt or feeling moral responsibility. The mind has all sorts of mechanisms for refusing to admit the truth to itself, and for making the perpetrator into another victim. The language of victimhood and fake-therapy flooded the trial – Huntley even talked about 'coping mechanisms' and 'closure'. In a grotesque displacement, the 'real' hidden self feels betrayed by its own actions.

Huntley feels he's not a 'pervert'. Maxine Carr said that when they discussed the issue of paedophiles, they both agreed they ought to be castrated and shot, and very possibly Huntley did believe this. Paedophiles are other people; rapists are other people; murderers are other people. It's hard for the mind to know itself as wicked. It tells itself a different story, keeping the darkness at bay. Week after week, Huntley listened to what he had done and didn't collapse. An accident, he said. Not something he did, but something that happened. What would it mean for him to accept that what he has done is also what he is? How could he possibly live with this knowledge? In prison, Ian Huntley will be in solitary confinement and on suicide watch. Even his adored mother has abandoned him now. The celebrity days are over; all the ghastly pleasure and the horror. The con man is alone with his mind. Whether he stays alive, or whether he kills himself, his future is deathly.

Did she know?

Maxine Carr stepped into the witness box after Huntley left it. Slender in her dark suit, with her mop of reddish-brown hair and slightly flat and shiny face, with small, bright eyes, she was a woman who looked like a child. She seemed younger than her years, as well; girlish in her unfocused garrulousness, her willingness to please. When she was asked a question, she would take a deep breath and set off, releasing a flood of undiscriminating details. As she talked, her nervousness evaporated. She liked chatting. She liked telling little anecdotes, recalling conversations. Every so often she giggled. She seemed not to realise the gravity of her situation. She appeared quick rather than clever; eager rather than bright. As an acting assistant teacher, she had been criticised for not keeping her distance from the pupils – she was too anxious to be liked and to be one of them to have appropriate authority. She liked attention; she wanted to be understood by the court and the world. She needed her story to be told (even now, all these months after, she has claimed to want to 'clear her name', not understanding that history has moved on.) And at first – as her lawyer led her through the rehearsed questions – she was indeed rather endearing: a sweet and trusting creature who'd stumbled into a nightmare and kept on thinking she would wake up. She was a girlish woman in a narrow world that had been suddenly flooded with a deeper darkness she could not comprehend

Gradually, however, another side of Maxine Carr also emerged, like the invisible backing that makes a mirror shine. She was tough; she was savvy; she was bitterly resentful; she was filled with a narcissistic self-pity that rhymed with Huntley's own. 'Why me?' was the subtext, not 'why them?'

She was quick to blame and slow to show any guilt; quick to forgive herself and condone her own small-minded motives. In this way, she was no different from most of us, who feel ourselves misunderstood by the world and for whom the allure of fame and celebrity is the promise of being recognised at last for the buried person we actually are. And after all, she wasn't guilty of much. She simply thought of herself and thus made herself blind – blind to the clues, and blind to the grief of others.

He had spoken of her in the present tense, but she shoved him into her past. He had called her 'Maxine' ; she called him 'Mr Huntley', 'Ian Huntley', 'that man' and, once, sobbing and gesturing, 'that thing'. 'I'm not going to be blamed for what that thing in the box has done to me,' she said, before adding, almost as an afterthought, 'or those children.' The story she told was one that was finished with: a grim chapter that she would not understand.

***

Maxine Carr was in Grimsby when Jessica and Holly died. Although during her time in Holloway, women leaned from their cells to abuse her, she was not charged with murder, only with perverting the course of justice and – although she admitted to systematically and repeatedly lying in order to provide her former boyfriend with an alibi – she pleaded not guilty because she insisted, over and over again, that she 'knew' Huntley could not have killed the girls. 'Those girls walked away from my house,' she told the police when pressed. She claimed she was protecting him from the past, and the allegations of rape that had propelled him into a nervous breakdown, not from the present or the future. She said that she lied because she loved him and because it never crossed her mind to suspect him of anything so terrifying and 'disgusting'. And, under cross-examination, she cried out that she lied because she was his victim as well: 'I was pushed into a corner...', 'I had no choice...', 'You have no idea what kind of relationship I had with that man...', 'I've a mind of my own now that I've had sixteen months away from him...' She spoke both the language of romance – 'I loved him' – and the language of betrayal. The reality was a bit more tarnished, of course. Photographs taken on the evening that the girls died show Maxine kissing a stranger across a pub table, while her approving mother looked on. Simple love is the tale we tell ourselves and others to cover up the more compromised truth about our lives.

Huntley was a stranger – a child abuser and murderer with a friendly face – but Maxine Carr transfixed us for different, more mundane reasons. How much did she know? This was the question that obsessed us, and with the same evidence everyone had a different, stubbornly held answer. Nothing, we said. Or, something. Or every-thing, of course, because look at that duvet shoved in to the washing-machine while she was away; look at the clean-up the slob-of-the-century Huntley had done in her absence, who never usually lifted a plate into the sink if he could help it. She knew but wouldn't let herself know, we said. She was willingly blind. And the question we asked about her was the question we asked about ourselves – would you have known, in her position? Would you, could you, ever suspect the person you lived with of something so foul, or would you hold on to your belief in the face of all the facts, until there was nothing left to hold on to? For once it takes hold, distrust spreads like rust. And if you suspected, would you then protect him?

Of course, there is the ubiquitous, more familiar question with which we rehearse this unimaginable one – if your partner was having an affair, would you suspect? Or: when your partner was having an affair, *did* you suspect? Many of us can now look back and ask ourselves with incredulity how we did not know what was so glaringly obvious. How could we have missed the sheets in the washing-machine, the endless showers, the strange behaviour. But, of course, it is easy read history backwards.

In fact, Maxine Carr admitted in court that 'sex' had briefly crossed her mind, when she saw that Huntley had changed the bedding. But not sex with a ten-year-old; not murder of the two girls who had wanted to be her bridesmaids. Even when she knew they had been in her house, up the stairs, into the bathroom and bedroom; even though she knew that Huntley had been charged before with sexual assault, she still looked stubbornly away from the truth.

Many people refuse to believe that she could see everything that was under her nose, and yet still remain blind to its meaning. Yet there is a famous psychological experiment where volunteers are asked to look at a video in which a ball is thrown between two people. The volunteers' job, they are told, is to count the number of times the ball is passed. Half way through the film, a figure dressed up in a gorilla suit steps in front of the camera and bangs its chest several times before disappearing again. After the experiment, the volunteers are asked the result of their count. Once they have given their answer, they are asked if they noticed anything strange about the experiment. In nearly half of the cases, they have noticed nothing, although to anyone watching the video who knows in advance what so surreally occurs, this seems almost impossible to credit. But the volunteers are not looking for anything strange; they are specifically and obediently looking at the ball and thus screening out whatever interferes with their concentration. The experiment shows what we already know – that we choose not to notice many things in our day-to-day life that do not seem necessary or relevant. We have to, or we would not function. We see what we want to see, and disregard the rest. Maxine Carr was a great disregarder.

In her avid and continual cleaning, perhaps we can see a symbolic need to scrub away the nasty stains of life and reality. She was fastidious, and didn't like dirt at all. Not one bit. In court, some of her most resentful comments were reserved for Huntley's sloppy domestic habits. He might be a murderer but he was also – her nose wrinkled up – a *slob*. There were crumbs around the sofa where he lay, drinking beer and watching telly. He didn't notice, but she did. Maxine Carr said that cleaning was her 'job' and duty as a woman, especially when she had no other work to do. When Ian Huntley went out to the school, she stayed home and set to with a duster and an iron and a mop, with the Bleach and the Flash and the Shake 'n' Vac, the Vanish and the Dyson vacuum cleaner. Top to bottom, week in and week out. Wash those curtains; get a narrow scrubbing brush along the cracks in the tile. Make dirty life clean again, until Huntley's smart Brushers or his canvas trainers (bearing specks of dirt that would trace him back to the site of the Lakenheath ditch) tramped all over it once more. She washed herself, as well – long baths and showers, a scrupulous cleanness, especially when she was menstruating. And she starved herself back into the shape of a girl. One day, she said, she wanted to be a wife and a mother.

***

We will never know what was going on inside Maxine Carr's head over those days and weeks, while she scoured the house, erasing clues of the crime in the process, or lay beside Huntley at night (letting herself 'be stroked', as her lawyer said, in one of those peculiar locutions used in the courtroom and nowhere else). Perhaps she herself does not know any more: there is a porous wall between fantasy and fiction, reality and image in this case.

In front of the television camera during the great search for the missing girls, she proved herself a dazzling liar – not simply repeating and improving her performance, but improvising so as to appear completely natural and authentic. It seemed to me that she probably convinced herself with her performance, and thought she actually was the woman she was so fluently pretending to be: the loving girlfriend, the giggly, popular teacher, the sweet betrayed victim. For many, this proved her guilt; but it could equally demonstrate her capacity for self-deception. In front of the cameras, in front of the judge and jury and journalists, she could turn into the woman she wanted to be, the woman she felt she really was but who had never previously had the chance to shine – a celebrity, all eyes on her. Even in prison, after the verdict, she wanted to sell her story and 'clear her name'. The world had not seen the woman she believed herself to be. She had not been – to use the horrible common parlance – validated. Although 'How much did she know?' was always the question, we'll never have the answer now, and now we should leave her alone rather than go baying after her.

In court, Maxine Carr spoke of her new freedom from Huntley – she had *thought* she loved him, she said, but that was because during their time together she was not free but in his thrall. What she had thought of as love was actually servitude. Only when she had been some months away from him could she at last see her life clearly and recognise that their relationship was a fraudulent copy of love. As people found her guilty by association, she struggled to prove her innocence by rupturing all connections between them. She thought she loved him but in fact she hated him; she thought he loved her, whereas he simply controlled her; she thought she knew him through and through whereas in fact his real self – the terrifying, paedophile self that assaulted and murdered two little girls – lay buried under his charming surface. She had thought she was at the centre of an ordinary domestic tale, but all the time she was in the margins of a dark and nasty thriller.

***

Not guilty of aiding an offender, said the jury of Maxine Carr, but guilty of perverting the course of justice. Three and a half years, said Justice Moses, condemning her self-ishness and her glib lies that added to the torment of the family.

Maxine Carr's name has been linked to Huntley's; her future, as her counsel Michael Hubbard said before the sentencing, has been 'blighted'. She has been hounded, vil-ified, compared repeatedly to Myra Hindley, not only by the inmates of Holloway Prison where she was kept after her arrest, but also by newspapers. She has been done over – made into a primitive scapegoat and given the full trash treatment. Words used about her were the same ones used about Saddam Hussein. Yet she was convicted of lying, not of complicity – of ignorance and misplaced loyalty, not of wickedness.

When in February, she applied to be released early from prison under an electronic tagging system, she was refused. She had been put forward for release by the governor of Holloway prison, Ed Willetts, but was turned down by the Prison Service chief, Martin Narey, whose decision was believed to have been made under the powers recently introduced to allow the refusal of an application if it could 'undermine public confidence' – and there was instant speculation that these new powers were introduced by

David Blunkett specifically in an effort to keep Carr in prison for as long as necessary.

Narey, in his letter to Maxine Carr, explained that his refusal was based both on concern for her own safety at the address at which she proposed to live (her mother's house in Grimsby) and the larger 'issue of public confidence'. He wrote that, 'Although not charged with murder, your offence was considered so closely related to the events surrounding the murder of the two girls and the police investigation that followed that you were tried jointly with Ian Huntley. Your conviction for conspiring with Ian Huntley to pervert the course of justice connects you indelibly with this case and with the public outcry that has accompanied it. For this reason, the possibility of your early release on HDC [home detention curfew], so soon after the trail has ended, would undermine public confidence in the HDC scheme.'

In other words, this had nothing to do with the law, everything to do with the power of public opinion (in a *Sun* poll, readers had voted by an overwhelming 95 per cent for her to stay in prison; many don't want her ever to be let out). And this was 'public opinion' in a peculiar sense. Narey commissioned no surveys to assess the views of ordinary people. His decision can only have been based on a reading of the newspapers which themselves had whipped up an inaccurate rabble-rousing campaign against Maxine Carr. This indelible connection with Huntley's crime had no basis in law. A decision on sentencing had apparently been made according to the prejudices of the popular press.

It gets worse. In the week before Maxine Carr was let out of prison, she appeared in court again to face charges of fraud, to which she pleaded guilty. Crowds with placards bearing legends such as 'Child-killer' protested against her and against her imminent release.

Anger was fed by the news that millins of pounds were being spent on her protection (as a fairly typical letter in the *Daily Mail* put it, 'to spend £15 million to protect the life of a convicted criminal... is a crime in itself... Maxine Carr should be relased, if need be, like any other prisoner. Give her what she is entitled to – not a penny more, not a penny less – and leave her to her just desserts. That is the civicilised way to deal with the matter.'

Maxine Carr's release has taken place strictly in adherence with the rules. She was sentenced to three and a half years for conspiracy to pervert the course of justice, and she has been in prison since August 2002. The fact that so much money has to be spent on keeping her safe from the baying crowds who want – what? Revenge? – is hardly her fault.

Many of those who are so outraged at the cost of her new identity are precisely the people whose demonisation of the young woman made it necessary.

Even some of the people who have been arguing her corner have hardly helped her case. Beatrix Campbell said that Carr should not be punished for what she'd done because, like Myra Hindley and like Rosemary West, she had been 'in thrall' to Huntley. Set aside the dubiousness of an argument that says that women are not responsible for what they do, the linking of Carr's name to West's and – repeatedly – to Hindley's, is ludicrous. She lied; they tortured and killed.

In one sense only is it useful to think about the case of Myra Hindley. In both cases, public and press sentiment were further tainted by misogyny. A woman connected with murder becomes monstrously unnatural. In the corruption of objective, clear-eyed justice, there is a way in which Maxine Carr can be compared to Hindley.

When Hindley and Ian Brady were found guilty at the Chester Assizes in 1966 – she of two murders, he of three – capital punishment had only recently been abolished. If the trial had been held the previous year, they would have been put to death and our image of Hindley would have been fixed into unmoving myth: the dyed blond hair and the staring eyes; implacable, ghastly, with a name like something out of a blood-chilling playground chant. Instead, she remained behind bars for 36 years, until her death in November 2002. Alive, she still haunted us. Hatred for her, kept fresh by repeated applications for parole, never faded. Her bleached-out photograph became like a nightmarish inversion of Andy Warhol's Marilyn Monroe. A portrait of her face by Marcus Harvey that was shown at the 'Sensations' show, was considered a blasphemous image. Even after she died, police had to guard her corpse, as if it still had power to harm – like radioactive dust.

Alongside all the terrifying images – the stony face, the tape played in court so that people heard a little girl being killed – there's another image: a woman with dark brown hair and a thin, calm face, growing older. Hindley – like Rosemary West – was an impressionable teenager when she met the dysfunctional Brady, a young man with a penchant for Nazi literature and pornography, and a fondness for torturing animals. She became caught up in his brutal fantasy world, where the lines between fantasy and reality, sex and violence, unravelled. Before she met him, she was a well-behaved Catholic girl; after she escaped him, she returned to the Catholicism of her childhood and considered herself washed clean of her monstrous past. She was, she says, under his spell (much as Carr later said that she was in thrall to Huntley, and wasn't 'herself'; whatever being your self actually means), and without him she would have led an ordinary, decent life. This was always her defence: that she was a coerced, weaker woman. And yet it is Hindley's face and name that we remember, not her lover's.

Over and over again, we were forced by Hindley to ask the question: can you change so that you become someone else entirely, struggling free from the ghastly wreckage of the past? Can you be forgiven? Can you forgive yourself? Can you be reborn? Generally, the public tended to think not . She had served her time; she had been a model prisoner; but nevertheless they wanted her to rot in prison (in the absence of capital punishment) and then to rot in hell. There could be no redemption.

And because of public opinion and the enduring power of the victims' family, successive Home Secretaries thought not too. There, all resemblance ends. Maxine Carr was a foolish, glib young woman who looked the other way.

**

I remember during the trial of Rosemary West asking a psychiatrist if she thought that West would ever be able to face up to what she had done. She replied: 'What would that mean? If she truly faced up to it, she would have to kill herself, or go mad.'

In our daily lives, we all protect ourselves against the knowledge of ourselves, and build up complicated defences against truths we cannot bear. We all have stories of ourselves we hang on to and repeat, in order to persuade ourselves of their truth and to keep at bay the chaos that lies beneath. And yet at the same time we tend to believe in a buried 'true' self that the outside world cannot perceive or understand. Part of the struggle of modern, post-Freudian life is both to present ourselves as a coherent narrative and at the same time to find recognition for the hidden and authentic self that lies between the lines.

In court Maxine Carr and Ian Huntley both spoke in the voice of the misunderstood and unrecognised victim. Maxine Carr had some reason for this – but the stern faces of the parents at the back of the court, and the iconic photograph of Jessica and Holly with their glowing, happy faces, always felt like a rebuke to her self-pity. Huntley's self-pity was murkier. Yet it seems perfectly credible to me that he believed himself and his ludicrous tale of an accident. He believed it because he had to believe it – anything else would have destroyed any sense he had of himself. His internal structure would have collapsed entirely, leaving only a rubble of hellish despair. He was not, in his own mind, 'a paedophile' – paedophiles are other people; dirty old men, not handsome young ones with the capacity to charm and please. Nor did he think of himself as a murderer. Murderers are other people. He thought of himself as unlucky – by chance, on that day, two young girls walked by his door. By chance, his rage had been triggered. Things happened. A terrible nightmare bloomed by pure bad luck and suddenly he was there, with two dead bodies lying on the carpet. Say the words often enough and you start to believe them: I wasn't myself. My mind went blank. It was an accident. It wasn't me. It wasn't the me that's the real me.

So Ian Huntley bemused us in court by talking about 'Kev' – the same Kev whose daughter he had killed and who sat a few feet away from him. He talked about how he had said sorry to Kev ('I didn't realise it was your daughter') as if he had no sense at all of the grotesque inappropriateness of his covert apology. He explained – without wincing at the monstrous weirdness of his personal vanity at such a moment – how he had changed out of his smarter shoes (his 'Brushers') before leaving the house to dump the bodies of his victims, because he didn't usually wear his Brushers outdoors. He was distanced from his crimes, because he felt his crimes were distanced from him, aberrations in his narcissistically shallow world.

**

Is what you do separate from what you are? Christianity and then the culture of therapy tells us that it is. Motive, intention and contrition count for much; we can sin by thought alone and be redeemed by sorrow. Are we the sum of our actions, or are we much more than that? Is evil simply an action, a verb, or is it lodged somewhere inside us, like dirt? For Huntley, the 'real' self, whom nobody else understands, was betrayed by his actions in the outside world.

Much is written about guilt: the way we feel it excessively or inappropriately; the way it eats into us; the way we carry around guilt like Protestant baggage, unable to shake off our past. But what about lack of guilt? Huntley's inability to take any kind of moral responsibility for what he did has a psychopathic quality, but Maxine Carr's has a simply and disconcertingly human one which most of us will recognise in ourselves as well.

Years ago I watched a television documentary about people who had been on the periphery of the Nazi atrocities in the Baltic states – not the monstrous villains of history, who chose to do evil, but the petty ones. Neighbours who'd looked the other way; guards who'd obeyed orders;

good citizens who, in the wrong place at the wrong time, became bit-part actors in terrible crimes. The film-maker had interviewed dozens of them and they all said things like: you weren't there so you don't understand what it was like; I was just obeying orders; I didn't know anything; I did what I was told; it wasn't my fault....

Only one man, an interpreter who'd tried to warn the people whose words he was translating of what was gong to happen to them, showed guilt, weeping when he spoke of what he'd done. The man who'd behaved the best felt the worst about himself. The others were implacably determined to resist blame for their actions. Like the volunteers in Stanley Milgram's classic experiment in obedience, they easily gave up moral responsibility to others. What would you do? they asked. None of us know what we would do until we are tested, and most of us have the moral luck to never be tested. Perhaps the virulence of public reaction to people like Maxine Carr, to Mary Bell, to the two ten-year-old boys who killed James Bulger, stems from the question. The more scared we are of being like them, the more we are viciously self-righteous, unimaginatively unforgiving. We hate Maxine Carr, even now when we know that she was in no way involved in the girls' death, because in her narrow focus and her shallow, self-serving fantasies, she may just be a bit like all of us and we want to reject that notion, pelt it away with eggs, spit it away with obscenities.

**

On April 5 2004, 5 College Close, the caretaker's house in which Jessica and Holly were murdered, was razed to the ground. For two years, it stood as a reminder of the crime – though the windows and doors were boarded up, and inside the rooms were stripped, only labels left behind to identify where things had once been. It took less than five minutes for the twenty-ton bulldozer to crush the fence, chomp up the roof and then tear up the walls, reducing the house to to dust. There will be no memorial in its place – neither family wanted that. The principal of Soham College, Howard Gilbert, said that there would be relief in the village and 'a sense of lightness'. The local firm that carried out the demolition signed a confidentiality agree-ment to ensure that none of the debris from the house should find its way onto the souvenir market. The rubble will be crushed into dust and disposed of at a number of secret locations. Huntley's garage was also destroyed, as was the school hangar where the girls' Manchester United shirts were found. The sites will be either landscaped or simply concreted over.

This is one of the traditions that has grown up with notorious English murder addresses. Rillington Place, the scene of Christie's murders, was renamed and then demolished. Fred and Rosemary West's house at Cromwell Street was replaced by a garden. It's as if every solid object associated with these murders was contaminated and remains toxic, as if something has seeped into the soil.

Care and care less

In the year 2002-03, Jessica Chapman and Holly Wells were two of the one thousand and forty-eight homicides in England and Wales. What about the other one thousand and forty six? Here is an example of a homicide that never made the front pages. It barely made it into the national newspapers.

At the same time as the Soham trial on the same Monday morning in late November, in another court at the Old Bailey, Ian Madden was scheduled to stand trial for the murder of his ex-wife, Lynn Burgess, the mother of his two small children. Lynn was the great friend of my sister-in-law, Norma French; the two had known each other since their childhood in Scotland and had remained very close to each other, sharing a house at one point, and turning to each other in times of difficulty. Lynn had died in the early hours of December 15th, 2002. She was thirty-eight; her son Ross was five and her daughter, India, was only just one.

I look at her photograph, standing at a fortieth birthday party in a bright blue dress. She is slim, with abundant, curly dark hair, sallow skin and a direct and radiant smile. She looks very happy and very kind; very alive. 'Beautiful,' says Norma, 'and with a beautiful nature too. There was no badness in her; she was good through and through. She was always calm, always mild-mannered, always generous – she saw the best in everyone.' She was very creative and had a wonderful eye: she loved sewing; she made all the things for her wedding. And she wrote poetry in her spare time, including the poem she wrote for her wedding day, standing up to recite it in front of everyone.

Lynn Burgess grew up in Scotland, studied French and German, then at twenty-one moved south – first to Cambridge, where she worked with an accountancy firm, and then a year or so later to London. For several years she had a steady boyfriend called Jake ('the best fellow that ever happened to her,' friends say), and seemed contented with her life.

Then, in 1991, she met Ian Madden, an Indian IT programmer several years her senior, rich and charming.

Jake didn't stand a chance. 'He swept her off her feet; she was completely taken in by him. A lot of us were.' Madden had been married before (at his trial he claimed that he and his first wife separated because she refused to have children, but the reason given on the divorce papers was an affair that Madden had had with his secretary, and his wife – who was too scared to give evidence against him – says the relationship was also verbally and physically violent).

In November 1993, Lynn moved in to Madden's smart home near Canary Wharf, and in 1994 they married. Even then, Lynn had had warning signals – on one holiday, during a heated argument, he had flung her out of their hotel room naked. Later, she told her mother, Betty Burgess, that by the time she was on her honeymoon she already knew that 'I had just made the biggest mistake of my life, Mum.'

Two years later, she became pregnant, and she stopped working. In February 1997 her son Ross was born. Lynn always knew that Madden had been abused himself as a child; she was aware of the seeds of violence in him and was anxious about the pattern being repeated with their own son. And after the birth of Ross, their life together darkened considerably. Both of them were cast down and depressed. They went to Relate together and then were both prescribed Prozac by their GP – though Lynn had never before been depressed. It seems more likely to her friends that she was *oppressed*. Her doctor was trying to cure her of inner troubles whereas what was wrong was her life in which she no longer a free young woman but a worn-down and virtually imprisoned one. Her husband was an angry and a controlling man. He insisted that she stayed at home rather than return to work. He moved the small family from their London home to a house in Havering-atte-Bower, Essex, where she knew nobody. He chose the clothes she should wear and even, bizarrely, tried to make her look nearer his age by ordering her to dye her glorious dark hair grey (while he dyed his grey hair jet black). What's more, his vigilance was becoming claustrophobically possessive and paranoidly jealous: he would ring her up several times a day to check up on her, even calling the Customer Services when she was at Tescos, and was suspicious of any life she had away from him.

By late 2000, Lynn was telling her mother that Madden was putting pressure on her to have a second child, but she was uncertain and anxious about it. Betty Burgess remembers telling her that if her marriage was in difficulty, having a baby was not the wisest thing to do. She thought then that her daughter had things under control – but Lynn came off Prozac and got pregnant early in 2001. In November, India was born. Lynn, everyone agrees, was a wonderful and adoring mother, but by then she knew her marriage was over, although she didn't articulate this for several more months. One morning in April 2002, she told Norma, she woke up and could see the vicious circle that had trapped Madden now being passed on to her and her children. 'And I knew at last that I had to break it.'

At Easter, the four of them drove up to Scotland to visit her parents, David and Betty Burgess. Madden – who had had several road-rage incidents before – terrified her with his dangerous driving and his violent temper. They had a serious argument and as soon as they returned home, she went to her solicitors to start divorce proceedings.

Madden refused to move out of their home and begged her not to go ahead with the divorce. By then, he was self-employed, and he signed off on sick leave for eight weeks, so the estranged couple and their tiny children were together every moment of the day: he wouldn't let her out of his sight. On the evening of September 6th, three days after the decree *nisi*, and having failed to persuade her not to sign the decree absolute, he tried to strangle her. Maybe she would have died then, but five-year-old Ross threw a remote control at his father and checked him for long enough for Lynn to take her children and run straight to the police station. Madden was removed from the house and charged with common assault. He was sentenced to sixty hours of community service. Her stalwart, concerned parents moved down to Essex and stayed with their daughter for the next eight weeks. Every Sunday, they acted as the third party who would hand over the children to their father for his one-day of access.

'The old Lynn returned,' says Norma. She had been wretched and trapped and now she was not. Now she could see what he had put her through and for the first time she could be honest about it to family and friends, pouring everything out, looking back on the nightmare with a sense that only once she was out of it could she see what she had been through. She changed her name back to Burgess. She became interested in clothes again, and in her appearance. She started to talk about going back to work – she wanted to train to become a teacher. She took up French jive. Her life was suddenly wide open again and full of possibilities. Friends say that she was 'blossoming'.

At the end of November, after India's first birthday, David and Betty Burgess returned home to Scotland to prepare for Christmas. Lynn and her children were going to join them a few weeks later. On December 5th, she went out for a meal with a businessman whom she had met at her dance class – it was a casual date. The following Sunday, when Ross and India were with their father, she went for a walk with the same man, and invited him over for dinner on Saturday December 14th. Later, papers would call their relationship 'an affair', but really it was simply three innocent meetings, and who knows if it would have led anywhere. They never had the time to find out.

Ian Madden was an IT programmer and he was a violently jealous man. He had access to Lynn's hotmail account and, in the trial, computer experts showed that in the weeks after their separations he obsessively checked up on her, without her knowledge. On one single day he logged in to her account from the early morning through to the early hours of the following day, adding up to a total of 177 times – that's a call every few minutes. He knew all about her arrangements to have a man round for dinner. He had also bought a bugging device. Now he could track her and he could listen to her. On the night of the dinner, he drove his car to the house, sat outside and listened. At one in the morning, her date left Lynn, with her daughter India awake again and sitting on her lap. He drove away, and as he did so he noticed a car parked outside the house, with a man sitting in the driver's seat. He thought that this was odd at such a time of night, and doubled back to check up on him, but by the time he returned, the driver had gone, although the car was still there.

The driver had indeed gone from the car. He had got out and gone into the house, where Lynn must have still been sitting with India on her lap. Who knows what Lynn thought, what went through her mind? Who knows what India witnessed? Ian Madden strangled Lynn Burgess ('manual strangulation' was given as the cause of death). As she was throttled to death, she scratched him desperately along the cheek so that some of her nails were torn out, and with great presence of mind he cut the rest of her finger nails and then scrubbed beneath them, to destroy any evidence, although traces of his DNA still remained. Then he went to the garage and fetched a rope he knew was there, wrapped it round her throat from behind and, as forensic pathologists concluded, probably put his knee against her back and jerked hard on the rope, which later would be shown to have his blood on it. He made a noose, put it round her neck, and draped the other end over a beam and back down, in a cool-headed but ineffectual imitation of suicide. He left Lynn's body lying on the floor. Then he left the house, his dead wife, and his two tiny children who would – as the judge said later – inevitably find their mother's body later, and drove back to the house where he was staying.

He was probably up all night – it is known he checked his voice mail at four am. At any rate, he didn't change his blood-stained trousers before driving back to Havering-atte-Bower. It was Sunday, his day of access, and he was going to take his children to see *Jack and the Beanstalk on Ice*. He arrived at the house shortly after nine and said he saw 'a shape' through the window. He dialled the emergency services and then knocked on the door. Nobody came. He knocked again and at last his son let him in and together they 'discovered' the body of Lynn, lying on the floor tied with rope. There is a terrible gap in this story for we can't know what the children had been through during the hours they were alone in the house with their dead mother.

At midday, the police arrested him. Madden was the estranged husband; he had a nasty fresh scratch down his cheek. DNA linked him inextricably to the scene. His car had been seen. In court, he appeared nearly bald, with his once-dyed-jet hair white. He was impassive, and in spite of all the evidence against him he denied emphatically that he had killed his wife ('Christ no,' he said, when asked if he was guilty. 'Killing Lynn would be like killing my own children.') Like Ian Huntley, he waited until he knew the hard facts of the prosecution case before deciding on his own thin thread of a story which, though feeble, did enough to persuade at least some of the jury that he might not be guilty of murder but of manslaughter. They were unable to reach a verdict and the whole case had to be retried several months later. Once again, the parents had to sit through the ordeal. This time, there was a verdict: guilty. Judge Geoffrey Rivlin QC, said that the 'case represents a tragedy of unimaginable proportion to all concerned', and taking into account the aggravated nature of the murder, sentenced Ian Madden for life, with a minimum tariff of eighteen years. He would be an old man before he left prison; his children would be adults. Madden swayed in the dock at the sentence and his legs buckled as he was led away.

When the police found Lynn's body, noose around her neck, they could not understand why there was a knife lying beside her. Perhaps, they thought, she had been trying to protect herself; perhaps he had been intending to use it on her. It was many months before the reason was discovered, and it was not admissible at the trial since it was hearsay by a minor. Her five-year-old son Ross had put it there. He eventually confessed to his aunt, asking if a child could be sent to prison too, because he thought he might have killed his mother by mistake. When, all alone, he had come across Lynn lying dead on the floor, tied with rope, he had left the knife by her side so that she could cut herself free when she woke up. Children often do not understand that death is a one-way journey.

The children, stripped of both parents at once and having to come to terms with the fact that their father murdered their mother while they slept upstairs, are apparently doing well. They have loving family and friends to help them through. Their uncle and aunt are adopting them. Their grandparents are nearby and always at hand. Ross looks just like his father, and India is the spitting image of her mother, whose photograph stands on her bedside table, smiling joyfully at the little girl who will have no memories of her.

But although the verdict comes as a relief (they were all determined that Madden should never get his hands on his children), Lynn's parents and her friends remain haunted by the young woman, who should still be among them still. David and Betty Burgess talk about her all the time, remembering little things, dwelling on the vivid details of her life, never letting her fade but keeping her alive and present in their hearts. She was a grown-up, not a ten-year-old, but for her mother and father, she will always be their first born, their only daughter, their baby.

***

There are no difficult lessons to be learnt from Soham. It was simply that the police should keep their records more efficiently, references should be checked properly. (Incidentally, the government paralysed the education system in the weeks after Soham, while all references were checked – was a single person caught by all that?) But Lynn's death raises issues that are occuring all over Britain every day, involving our lukewarm reaction to violence against women. What was amazing, in this brutal, pre-meditated case of murder, was the apparent resistance of the first jury to convict Madden of murder: they came close to convicting him of manslaughter, a finding so absurd that it hadn't even been mentioned as a possibility in the course of the trial, even by the defence counsel. And in the second trial, the conviction was only obtained by a majority verdict. Under the English system, jurors are strictly forbidden to reveal what went on in the jury room, but the suspicion was felt by some observers that some male members of the jury may have felt some sympathy for a husband who was punishing his wife for leaving him.

Domestic homicides just don't have the emblematic quality of the death of the children. When children die, the tragedy is purer, like an essence of loss.

Jessica and Holly were only ten. Although the day before she was murdered, Holly had bought a bra, they were pre-pubescent little girls. This was crucial to our fiercely emotional response. We adored their innocence. There was no hint of sexuality about them; they were our little princesses, as the condolence cards said, sleeping sweetly now; they were angels; little lambs to the slaughter. While Ian Huntley was a man of unravelled and brutalising sexuality, whose past was a nasty catalogue of obscenities and abuses, they were flat-chested, eager-faced, unblemished and blameless: perfect victims. Like James Bulger (whom the media persisted in calling 'Jamie', to further emphasise his diminutive childishness) or Sarah Payne, they played an uncomplicated role in our imaginations, and unequivocally summoned up all the fears we have for our own children.

In the UK, a small handful of children (usually between five and eight) are killed by strangers every year. About ten times that number are killed by people they know, usually in their home and by members of their own family, while countless more are injured and abused there. But domesticity dampens down our interest. A domestic murder is less bizarre and it's more discomforting than a stranger killing; less terrifying and yet more disturbing. The clean contrasts of the Manichean universe is what we respond to: good versus evil.

On 14 November 2002 (just a few months after Jessica and Holly had been murdered, and the country had been gripped by collective grief and mourning), fourteen-year-old Adam Morrell was killed in Loughborough. The last Adam's family had heard from him was when he phoned his father, days before his death, to say that he was staying with friends.

These 'friends' were the ringleader, Matthew Welsh, the nineteen-year-old son of a policeman; Welsh's girlfriend, seventeen-year-old Sarah Morris; nineteen-year-old Daniel Biggs; and Nathan Barnett, in his mid-twenties. Unlike Holly and Jessica, whose moments leading up to their murder were accounted for minute by minute, in loving and poignant detail, we don't know how Adam spent his final days. What we know is this: the group had been drinking whisky, smoking cannabis and taking ecstasy that evening, and when Adam apparently threatened to inform the police about their drug use, they turned on him ('he was bringing us down,' said Sarah Morris; while Welsh claimed he was irritating them by 'going on about his girlfriend'). Adam curled up into a ball and wept piteously as they punched him, kicked him, stamped on him. He had boiling water mixed with sugar poured over his body. A pathologists said at the trial in Nottingham that the boy had suffered more than 280 injuries: one of the defendants described him as looking 'like an alien', and another said he was completely unrecognisable.

Then two of them played the game of paper-scissors-stone, to decide who would finish him off. Finally, the boy was strangled. Then the music was turned up in the small semi, to mask the sound of Adam's body being sawn into pieces.

The story becomes like a grotesque farce. Three days after Adam was beaten and tortured to death, a group walking by the Grand Union Canal in the town found a black plastic bag wrapped in silver tape and floating in the water. Inside, there was a severed arm. Then a woman found legs in another plastic bag. The head was discovered by police divers at the bottom of the canal. The clothes turned up at an electricity sub-station.

Matthew Welsh was sentenced to at least twenty years in prison. Sarah Morris was cleared of murder, but jailed for four years for deliberately attacking the boy. Daniel Biggs was cleared of murder and inflicting grievous bodily harm, but sentenced to two and a half years for conspiring to pervert the course of justice. Nathan Barnett, the twenty-seven-year-old, was ordered to be detained indefinitely in secure accommodation under the Mental Health Act, after he pleaded guilty to manslaughter on the grounds of diminished responsibility.

This story has a sickening meaning, speaking to us about how people can behave without any shred of humanity and still feel no remorse. If we want to understand human depravity and unimaginable cruelty, we should look at what happened to Adam and at the behaviour of his killers, who egged each other on to torture him, who played a game over his dying body. While Jessica's and Holly's tale is closed off in its own hermetically sealed, small-town world, Adam's story opens out onto a grim canvas of slaughter. Perhaps this is one reason why, while it was virtually impossible to remain ignorant about the tenderest details of the deaths of Holly and Jessica, most of us have never heard of this desolating case – precisely because it was loaded with unwelcome meaning. Through one individual's tragedy, we can glimpse the vast horrors of Rwanda, where neighbours raped, tortured and murdered neighbours; where rivers ran thick with blood in a feverish orgy of killing. We can glimpse the lynch mobs in Iraq, where small boys whooped delightedly round the strung-up corpses of Western construction workers or young men dragged their bodies through the dust – and, of course, where American soldiers tortured and humiliated the prisoners at Abu Ghraiv. People as animals – except animals don't take the same savage pleasure in torturing others. In her book on war criminals in the Hague (*They Would Never Hurt a Fly*), Slavinka Drakulic writes that 'the more I have occupied myself with the individual cases of war criminals, the less I believe them to be monsters'. Rather they are ordinary men and women. That is the horror. Ordinary people – people like us – turned into monsters.

There is another reason, just as close to home, why we cared so very much about the young girls, and not much at all about the slightly older boy. In the small handful of newspaper stories, photographs of the murdered teenager and of the gang who tortured and then killed and dismembered him, stare out at us. Adam is swarthy-skinned and unsmiling, tired smudges under his large, dark eyes. The three males in the gang have thin faces, buzz cuts and dull, defiant stares, while the one young woman looks surly and remote.

Adam had not been home for several days before he was killed. He was a young teenager, already cutting loose from his family and adrift, mixing with youths older than him, in a world of drugs and drink and mindless violence. He had left his childhood and had entered a murky world of provincial Gothic, where unspeakable things take place in dreary semis on the edge of town. He was not snatched out of a happy, picture-book world into horror; he wandered into that horror by himself. Adam isn't the kind of figure with whom we automatically and unequivocally identify, and neither did his parents invite the media into their hearts and homes. There is none of the poignant domestic detail in this as a story, so that pity never translates into empathy. It happened 'out there', in a squalid, brutalised world we don't want to imagine or understand. It doesn't remind many of us of our own lives and middle-class concerns. We don't take young Adam – just fourteen years old, tortured to death by people he called friends – to our hearts. There's only so much sorrow to go round.

We did notice Millie Dowler, the Surrey teenager who went missing in March 2002. Her attractive face beamed at us from front pages; there was national concern, a huge hunt. She was a girl. She was white. She came from a close, middle-class family in the suburbs. Her parents co-operated fully with the police, made anguished appeals for her return. There was a cute video of her singing at her ironing board. We knew what she stood for – decency, innocence, middle-class comfort. We understood Millie Dowler and so her appearance struck a chord. Martin Bright, who wrote a thoughtful, disturbing piece about all the cases we ignore in the *Observer* in December of that year, laid down the rules for 'the missing persons game. Don't be a boy, don't be black, don't be working class. As for persistent runaways, children in care or teenagers with drug problems... forget it.'

So, as Bright showed, we forgot Hannah Williams, the fourteen-year-old girl from Dartford in south-east London, who'd gone missing in April 2001, and whose decomposed body was found wrapped in tarpaulin in a disused cement works in Northfleet, opposite Tilbury docks. There had

been no national media attention given to her disappearance, though some local newspaper carried appeals, and
there was little given to her death – just a few lines in the
'news in brief' columns of newspapers, and then silence.
She didn't have the right profile. She wasn't middle-class.
Her mother was a single parent. and wasn't, the police
thought, 'really press conference material' . Hannah had
gone missing before. So she disappeared, like a little ghost
in the great ghost world of a hundred thousand children
who go missing every year.

And so we also forgot Daniel Nolan, the fourteen-year-
old boy who went missing on New Year's Day 2002 from
the seaside village of Hamble, Hampshire. He had been
fishing off the quayside with friends, something he often
did, and was last seen on his way to collect his gear, but it
was found where he had left it. He was apparently a grown-
up and responsible boy; he had no history of running
away; his disappearance was inexplicable. But he was a boy.
Fourteen-year-old boys don't push the same buttons as
fourteen-year-old girls.

And so we forgot the black children, the boys, the drug
addicts, the children from broken homes or with difficult
backgrounds, the working-class children, the badly-
behaved children, the children who had run away before.
There are children and children. Some are more like 'chil-

dren' than others, and childhood, it seems, has become a battleground for all our desires and our fears.

***

'When I was a child, I spake as a child, I understood as a child, I thought as a child; but when I became a man I put away childish things.' When is a child not a child? When does childhood end and this thing called adulthood begin? How do we know? When in November 1999 the glam rock star Gary Glitter was cleared of indecently assaulting a fourteen-year-old girl nearly fourteen years previously, the judge said: 'There is fourteen, and there is fourteen. Some fourteen-year-olds look like sophisticated young ladies and some fourteen-year-olds still look like little girls. You may wish to consider which category the girl was in....'

So many stories to confuse us: the eleven-year-old Swiss-American boy arrested when a neighbour saw him 'touching' his five-year-old sister, handcuffed, locked up for six weeks in a detention centre; the trial of the thirty-two-year-old teacher, Renate Williams, who'd been accused of having sex with her under-age pupil and who in turn had accused him of bullying her – so the traditional relationship of teacher and student, adult and child, was turned on its head; the girls of eleven, twelve, thirteen, made pregnant by their under-age boyfriends; the fifteen-year-old girl who gave birth unnoticed and stabbed her newborn baby to death; the pre-pubsecent drug users; the falling age of first sex, the hundred thousand runaways who dissolve into the doorways of our great cities... These are tales of sex, violence, unhappiness and confusion and they jar horribly with the way we like to imagine childhood, as a time of alluring and vulnerable innocence.

To be childlike, we think, is to be innocent and to possess a capacity for joy, immediacy, eagerness – the carefree sense of absolute possibility. Like Sarah Payne, running through the meadow; like James Bulger, putting his hand into the hands of his killers; like Jessica and Holly, skipping down the road together, towards their death.

When a child does not fit this image of innocence, we console ourselves and keep the story neat by demonising them. They can no longer be termed a 'child'; they've become something other. We recognise that adults can be cunning, lustful, greedy, deceitful and self-deceiving, sometimes cruel, often cowardly, burdened by their past. Yet we persist in imagining most childhood – at least, 'proper' childhood – as simple: not scared, not lonely, not ashamed, not hard and not disturbed. The idea of the innocence of children is tremendously alluring.

But, of course, childhood is a construct. It changes with our times. Until the middle of the eighteenth century, children seemed to be regarded as faulty mini-adults in need of correction. In the portraits of seventeenth-century painters like Van Dyck, they wear adult clothes, have shrewd, responsible expressions. Even babies have old faces. With the Enlightenment, images of children changed: in Rousseau's *Emile*, Wordsworth's child 'trailing clouds of glory', John Everett Millais's angelic infants in paintings such as 'Cherry Ripe' or 'Bubbles', the child is innocent and sanctified.

But now, childhood is a focus for our adult desires and our adult anxieties. Children occupy the same kind of place in our imagination that women did in the late Sixties and early Seventies. Women used to be regarded as the guardians of certain virtues – purity, warmth, naturalness, gentleness, stability. Feminism tore apart that myth, and instead children became our last false hope: emblems of goodness that was vulnerable, and of a purity that could be poisoned. Sara Payne, Sarah's mother, who has written about her daughter's murder – *A Mother's Story* – is an advertisement for this view. She says, 'I never could imagine Sarah as an adult... She was too innocent for this world.'

We are sentimental about children, we are scared of

them, we want them to stay young, we force them to grow up. We are confused. The line between adulthood and childhood used to be tyrannically drawn – like the Berlin Wall, the two states were denied to each other, and in the authoritarian zone, the adults were the oppressors. But now it's collapsed. Children step over its rubble and into the grown-up world prematurely. Adults step back into a state of culturally trendy immaturity. The creator of Teletubbies said not so long ago that childhood stopped at eight.

In February 1993 the ten-year-old Robert Thompson and Jon Venables took the two-year-old James Bulger from a shopping centre in Liverpool and after a walk of more than two miles, past dozens of passers-by, arrived at a railway line. There they kicked him, then battered him to death with bricks and an iron bar. There have been other child murderers of children, but the start of this one was caught on security camera so we could watch, over and over again, the face of the toddler in the crowd, the last sight of him being led away. It was like a fragment of a home movie, except it utterly subverted the home movie tradition of preserving only the happy memories of family life.

It was clear almost at once that Venables and Thompson had killed James Bulger. What the trial turned on was how responsible the two boys were for their crimes. At ten, is a child a moral being? (The fifteen-year-old boy that the teacher Renate Williams was accused of seducing was regarded in court as a child; Venables and Thompson, five years younger, were treated in court as adults). When the verdict was returned, many people expressed satisfaction (as well as saying that they should never walk free again).

Although several people spoke out vehemently against ten-year-old children being caught up in a grotesquely inappropriate legal system, the majority of the public thought that somehow the two boys had forfeited the right to be thought of as children at all. They were un-children; they were monsters – more monstrous, it seemed, than adults who killed, because more 'unnatural'. The revulsion we still feel when women rather than men commit murders became revulsion squared. The arresting officer said: 'You should not compare these boys with other boys. They were evil.' Evil ten-year-olds; evil caretakers; perfect victims.

We are caught between two ways of knowing children. Our cultural ideal is cutely sentimental (all those pictures and cards and posters and biscuit tins of adorable creatures with ringlets and dimples and maybe a single tear rolling down a rosy cheek). Today, about half of all advertisements show pictures of children – wiping their bottoms with the gentlest lavatory paper, wrapped in towels made soft by fabric conditioner, running in a field made free by some insurance scheme. We still cling to the Wordsworthian view of a child whose delicious body is innocent of adult sexuality and whose mind is a blank. This sweet image also holds the dark side of innocence, which is the inevitability of its loss and its change. Many of the Romantic writings about children are actually about adult dread of mortality: to look at a child who thinks they will live for ever means to think about growing up, growing old, dying.

And at the same time, our gaze is fearful and predatory and, under it, children have become erotically suggestive creatures. The blank space becomes the free space for adult fantasies. Childhood innocence suggests its opposite, violation. (So, in the 1990s, the Miss Pears girl, advertising soap, was withdrawn: her glowing innocence was considered dangerously alluring, an image for dirty old men to drool over). There is no subject as publicly dangerous as the naked child's body. In 1989, Robert Mapplethorpe – famous for photographs which depict subjects like a man clad in leather urinating into another man's open mouth – was prosecuted for two of his photographs showing small children. They are doing nothing, just standing in front of the camera. The US photographer, Sally Mann, takes pictures of her own children. Beautifully composed, artistically black-and-white, they simultaneously convey childhood innocence and adult sexuality. The children are often naked and always knowing – or is it us, the viewers, who are knowing? They gaze complicity at the lens, undoing our expectation of the family snapshot. A child flung out naked on a mattress should embody purity and peace – but in Mann's photo, her legs are apart, there is a stain between them. Urine? Semen? She evokes a prostitute in post-coital exhaustion. Totally sweet and not sweet at all; quite innocent and all used up.

At a deep level, we like to think of childhood as a kind of Eden, but we've filled Eden with coiled serpents. Though statistically we live in a safer world now than ever before, we see danger in every tree. We see what's there and what isn't there. We know too much about the fallen world. There are fathers who abuse their offspring. There are molesters outside the school gates. There are bullies in the playground. There are drugs around the corner. The more we desire to protect them, the more dangerous the outside world seems to our children – and so, the more we desire to protect them.

In the streets of Soham there are CCTV cameras now, to stop the very thing that has already happened and will never happen again – not there, anywhere, and not like that. There will be a different man and a different place. Parents hold their children by the hand more tightly; they don't want to let them go. Letting go means relinquishing them to a world where the next Ian Huntley might lurk. Soham, like every other village and town and even city in the UK, is a safe place, but it doesn't feel safe any more. Childhood doesn't feel safe any more. There are monsters abroad, and monsters in our head.

Grief and grief's ripples

In March, three months after Ian Huntley had been found guilty of murdering their daughter Holly, Kevin and Nicola Wells gave an extended television interview, in which they spoke of their experiences from the moment the girls went missing, through the torment of waiting, the discovery of the bodies, the police investigation, the trial, right up to the present, when everything was over except for the granite certainty of grief. They talked of their loss, and indeed they were two people clearly ravaged by it, as if they'd passed through fire. They had about them the charisma of suffering, set apart by their experiences.

Nicola Wells wanted to bury Holly with her favourite soft toy; at first Kevin Wells resisted because he could still smell his daughter on its fur. It made for a scarcely bearable spectacle. Indeed, one wondered why we were watching such close-up and intimate agony, and being given the tender, heart-wrenching details of parental love and parental loss: why they wanted to show their torment, and we wanted to hear and witness it.

Yet they did want to, and perhaps there was an element of keeping Holly fully alive by so kindling their own fire of grief. When they were talking about her, over and over again, she was still with them. When they were silent, she slid out of their lives again and left them with her haunting. Bereaved people – parents, lovers – often speak of the agony of grief, and yet the terror of letting it go. They don't want to forget the beloved one for an instant. They don't want to recover – such a term is meaningless, especially for a parent who has lost a child and for whom life is wrenched out of its natural order. Nicola and Kevin Wells were talking , were pouring out their souls – but to whom? To the interviewer; to us, the anonymous, invisible audience; to their daughter, who would never hear them again; to nobody and everyone? An act of therapy without therapy's hermetic structure, a howl into the abyss.

Kevin Wells is also writing a book about the ordeal, and will be paid around £500,000 for the serialisation rights to the story by the *Mail on Sunday*. It is portrayed as an act of catharsis – a way of dealing with otherwise overwhelming emotion. Leslie and Sharon Chapman, on the other hand, have been emphatic that they do not want to talk to the press and do not want to make any money from the media. ('We wish to make it clear that we have no desire to engage in discussion with any media outlets now or at any time in the future.')

So on the one hand, the more traditional British way of dealing with sorrow and personal trauma: silence, privacy and reticence, where both damage and healing are invisible, and where you are alone with your sorrow. And on the other hand, the new road of disclosure, confession, revelation, when doors that were once kept closed are opened and when personal lives are made public. The pilgrimage of pain. Which one is more helpful?

There is no doubt which most of us now believe is the more helpful or the healthier. While a kind of valourous stoicism used to be the British ideal when faced with suffering, the opposite is true today. For all the repeated exhortations to leave grieving families 'in peace' to 'come to terms with their loss', we hold in far greater esteem the disclosure of private pain and have even become suspicious of silence and reserve – as if silence (which used to mean depth) now points to chilly absence, and reserve (which used to mean a gallant dignity) now stands for repression. Those who don't speak must have something to hide; those who don't show their feelings must have stifled them.

There was a brutality about the old insistence on the stiff upper lip and the inviolable sacredness of the private realm. All manner of wrongs have been done in its name – the little boys marched off to boarding schools, still clutching their teddies, bullied and buggered and never saying a word because it wasn't the thing to blab and because they had learnt that growing up meant dealing with such things alone; young men condemned as cowards and even executed when they suffered traumatic shell shock in the trenches; children sexually abused; generations of men and women passing damage down the line; patterns repeating.

Things have changed and a culture that once celebrated reticence now celebrates openness and dwells on psychological pain. The boys who were sent away to school to weep beneath the itchy blankets have become men who acknowledge the damage of their past and try to repair it. The self – that secret, endlessly fascinating labyrinth through which we may travel and yet never arrive, scrutinise and yet never understand – is the great undiscovered land within each of us. The more we discover about the workings of the mind, the more mysterious the mind becomes to us.

Therapy persuades us to attempt to understand our

selves. Counselling teaches us that by shining a spotlight into the darkest corners of the mind, we may take away some of the terrors that lurk there, and tries to help us turn unbearable grief into bearable sorrow. Analysis holds out the promise that, with uncomfortable honesty and hard work, we can change the hard grain of our behaviour. Therapy makes us into the centre of our own lives, and gives us a narrative with which to track back through the formless mess of our lives. It gives us a shape and a story to tell to ourselves; lowers a grid onto chaos. Yet at the same time, in therapy, we try to read between the lines that we've already written about ourselves, or had written. Like religion used to, it offers us meaning. The emphasis is on the preciousness of the individual. The outside world falls away and you are alone with your self: the mind looking at the mind.

The task therapy sets is austere (we are made to face up to those things we have previously squirmed away from) but its underlying message is consoling, for it tells us we do not have to suffer, and it holds out the promise that we can be rescued from the demons that torment us. We can help ourselves; save ourselves.

It used to be the case that nobody was given counselling or psychological help after a trauma. Men who fought in the two world wars endured their horrors alone, or denied them alone, as if they were shames. They pushed them into the basement of their mind and shut the door, tried to get on with their lives – and some of them managed and some did not. Now, though, counselling is accepted as a necessary part of healing. Talking – opening up the door to that dark room – is deemed necessary and helpful. There is trauma counselling offered to every victim. A form letter offering it is sent out by police when you report a crime. At the King's Cross fire, every professional who dealt with the aftermath was offered help. At the West trial, journalists who sat through the weeks of grisly narrative were told they shouldn't hesitate to seek counselling. It's more or less taken for granted now that talking, opening up, helps; remaining silent, damming up, hinders. The Wells way, not the Chapman way.

Frank Furedi, professor of sociology at University of Kent and trenchant critic of the culture of therapy, is one of the many who disputes the helpfulness of grief counselling. Some experts consider that the shock and sorrow can be intensified rather than relieved by dwelling upon it – in other words, denial is a very useful tool; repression can be the most effective way of surviving tragedy. Furedi points to the example of Aberfan, where hundreds of people were killed in the landslide, many of them school children. Nobody was offered counselling and apparently the community dealt with it in an exemplary way, supporting and consoling each other, yet maintaining a privacy of grief and a stoicism of outlook; allowing the structure of their life to carry them through. The school reopened after a couple of weeks; men and women returned to work. After the heartbreak and terror, life continued as life has to; the unbearable was borne. Time doesn't heal, but time passes, day by day and then year by year. Thirty years later, on the anniversary of the disaster, the media invaded the small town and encouraged its inhabitants to relive the experience, to open up and explore the pain they suffered – to make their internal landscape public. This, Furedi argued, recreated the grief that had healed over. Or this, other experts argued, allowed the damage that had been sealed up and suppurating to be lanced. Who's right? Does the deliberate suppression of anguish damp it down (no oxygen means no flame), or does it create a hidden, poisoned wound? Talk or silence? It seems to depend on what metaphor you use.

Counselling and therapy after a trauma used to be for those at the eye of the psychological storm (like the devastated parents of Holly and Jessica), but now it reaches out to all those affected, however slightly, by the ripples of disaster. Not just the Chapmans and the Wells, not just the extended family, the friends, the fellow pupils; not just all those who knew the girls; but everyone in Soham, everyone in the UK even – 'trauma' was the word applied by the media to the nation at large during the great search for the little girls. 'Trauma' was the state many people diagnosed themselves as suffering after their bodies were found.

After the collapse of the World Trade Centre experts predicted that one out of five New Yorkers – about one and a half million people – would be traumatised by the tragedy and require psychological care. Several thousand grief and crisis counsellors arrived at the city. It was accepted as almost a duty for employers all over New York to provide counselling for their employees. 'Bottling up' was dangerous. And people wanted to help each other. In the *New Yorker*, Jerome Groopman, writing about 'The Grief Industry', describes how such counsellors generally use a debriefing method, developed by Jeffrey Mitchell, a graduate student at the time, which takes place between twelve and seventy-two hours after a catastrophe (before that, people are too 'numbed', and after, they have begun to 'seal over'). In Groopman's account of the debriefing after September 11, he describes how, according to a participant, the people who broke down, really cried, were the people who had not been close to the event or personally affected by it. Yet over 99 per cent of participants said the counselling was beneficial to them. Was it really?

Over the past few years, there have been several surveys into the efficacy of grief and trauma counselling. Most have had what Groopman calls 'discouraging results'. Some researchers claim that debriefing, asking people to vent their feelings and relive their experiences, actually slows or impedes recovery. Groopman cites one study of burn victims which found that the patients who received debriefing were much more likely to report post traumatic stress than those in a control group. Humans are infinitely suggestible. Telling their story over and again will give them memories they didn't have, give them sadness they had not experienced, show them things they did not ever see. The imagination joins up the dots.

Scientific studies in the main seem to suggest that after a trauma most people are resilient and will recover over time, with or without help, while a small percentage require professional help (and many of these have a greater risk because of things like childhood abuse, a dysfunctional family background, a pre-existing psychological disorder). 'Abnormal' behaviour after a catastrophe or a sudden bereavement is only normal after all – part of the mind's struggle to heal itself and to come to terms with what has so suddenly happened. Insomnia, flashbacks, extreme shock – these are part of the self's mechanisms. Grief is part of the human condition, and so, it is argued, the whole notion of debriefing and counselling is constructed around the false idea that trauma causes damage – that we are all psychologically vulnerable and in need of outside help to get us through the pain of life.

Of course, counselling, therapy, analysis, all the many talking cures, cannot be contained in the discrete room where the talking and listening take place. It has dramatically spilled into the culture, seeping into even the most unexpected corners. Politics and rationality give way before the flood of personal confession. The language of emotional pain pervades our world. Furedi, in his *Therapy Culture: Cultivating Vulnerability in an Uncertain Age* lists some of them: damage, scars, vulnerability, healing, stress, depression, compulsion, addiction, mid-life crisis, trauma, closure (as in 'traumatised Soham seeking closure'), self-esteem. Low self-esteem, says Furedi, has become the favourite diagnosis for the insoluble problem of the human condition (in 1980, in a survey of three hundred newspapers, the term was not used at all; in 2000 it was used 3,284 times; Oprah Winfrey said it was the most over-riding concern of our times).

The concentration on what he calls 'emotional deficit', has, Furedi argues, brought about an intense sense of emotional vulnerability. There is, he says, a concentration on emotional deficit (self-esteem, he argues, really equals low self-esteem), which is like an 'invisible disease' undermining our lives. The huge increase in (reported) psychological depression – for those born before World War One it was one per cent; before World War Two, five per cent; during the Sixties, fifteen per cent – is, says Furedi, not simply a recognition of pain which was previously repressed, but an actual result of the cultural imagination of trauma, and the pathologising of our emotional responses to the pressures of life. There has been a huge growth in stress-related illnesses. The events we used to take for granted are now regarded as worrying. Pupils as young as four can be offered counselling; some schools set up help lines for students entering secondary school; giving birth has come to be seen as traumatic rather than simply an extraordinary-ordinary experience through which almost every woman passes; there is even bereavement counselling when a pet dies. This is what Furedi calls the 'promotion of the diminished self', a self that is fragile and in constant requirement of therapeutic help.

When Jessica Chapman and Holly Wells disappeared, when their bodies were found in the Lakenheath ditch, the nation felt itself traumatised, shocked, wounded and in mourning. What happened with Diana's funeral, what happened with Sarah Payne's murder, happened again. Their was a mass mobilisation of collective grief and of collective anger. The crowd that grieved and wept was the crowd that shouted and threw eggs at the Maxine Carr.

It's been often said that the emotionally charged, self-scrutinising therapy culture of today is a response to the waning of religion and of politics. We are not a secular age, so much as a post-secular one; not an enlightened but a post-enlightened one. Religion has not been replaced by science and reason so much as by emotionalism and a kind of needy, vague mysticism, a dissatisfied sense of spiritual absence. The decline of religion has meant the decline of meaning and magic, which we have rediscovered in the troubling complexity of the human mind. In our own psychology we have found new ghosts, new mysteries and a new sense of enchantment and heroic pain. Where once we turned outwards (to God and the church, to progress and politics), now we turn inwards, in an act of collective narcissism. Our world view is now largely therapeutic and centred on the self, that vast and undiscovered world of desire and fear. We attend to the single self, not to others. We judge people by the feelings they display rather than the ideas they hold. We need an audience for validation, and the admiring attention of others. The world is, as Christopher Lasch says in his important book *The Culture of Narcissism*, the mirror for our grandiose individuality. Robbed of its own richness, it becomes 'thinly populated' and un-nourishing. Reality, as Susan Sontag writes, comes to seem 'more and more like something we are shown by cameras'. In photographs and in videos we find out who we are. Celebrities seem more 'real' than ordinary people, while at the same time they are obviously brittle concoctions hiding the inner truth under the glossy surface.

In our hungry, unsatisfying self-absorption, suggests Lasch, we may be plagued by anger, restlessness, boredom, discontent, hidden and seething anger, and a sense of inner emptiness. Here, the pathological narcissism of Ian Huntley looks like a concentrated and toxic version of the general narcissism of the modern world, and indeed Lasch believes that we may commonly find the narcissism of someone like Huntley, in a subdued form, in society in general. The redemption of religion is no longer on offer; we feel let down by politics and the heady promises of the Sixties and Seventies. Therapists promise us salvation, though therapy is not like religion, which looks outward at the community of suffering. It's a lonely business, subjective salvation for ourselves alone, and we're not thinking about how to be good, but how to be happy.

The popular-therapy culture encourages us to disinter and scrutinise our own private pain, to trace and understand it. The story we tell to ourselves becomes a tale of suffering and of survival, until, bit by bit, the mere fact of suffering comes to seem like heroism. Then, of course, everyone can be a hero in their own life: there's a great democracy in this seductive language of feeling, which is available to everyone and in which everyone has an equal stake. We can all be victims if we want (bet my child birth was worse than yours), and most of us know the allure of being one. Consider the books about personal pain; the celebrities' confessions of past suffering; the diaries of illness and death.

What we used to do in solitude (with the priest, with the doctor, with the counsellor, with our closest friends) we now do in public, through the media whose pages are filled with tales of tragedy and endurance. People turn to newspapers to tell their stories and to be understood and recognised at last. They are telling their stories to the world and their own selves. They are confessing in a Godless age, unburdening their souls. And interviewers – like myself, many times – are eager to crack tough subjects open and let secret disturbance and frailty leak out. The things they don't want to speak about are the things we most want to hear. Distressed revelation is a mark of authenticity.

Victims talk and we listen. When Kevin Wells speaks of his grief, we fall silent (there were no advertisements during the lengthy television interview, as if it would be disrespectful to break into the tormented flow). We want a glimpse into other people's private hells; want to imagine for a while those things we most dread. Contact with the victim confers a touch of greatness on us, like the crowds who held on to the hem of Jesus' cloak.

***

Beware what you wish for; it might come true. In the Seventies and Eighties, one mantra of feminists, sickened by the gap between private lives and public ones, was 'the personal is the political'. Well, we've got what we asked for. Feelings displace actions: we leave flowers at the scenes of road accidents, sign books of condolences, add names to meaningless on-line petitions, remain silent for one minute or two or five, wear ribbons, feel empathy, share pain – and often, do nothing more. Politics shrivel under this intense emotionalism.

There are people who argue sternly against the newly open, emotional, victim-led culture as an infantilised, shallow, hypocritical and self-pitying version of real self-knowledge. They are firmly on the side of enlightened reason, of stoicism and irony. They mercilessly mock the crowds that weep for strangers. And there are people who eloquently snub the super-rationalists; for them the term 'therapy culture' is a radically liberating one, opening up lives that were hitherto chilly and repressed. Then there are the rest of us who are stuck in a muddle between the two, sincerely touched and yet simultaneously disturbed by our own instinctive emotional reaction; part of the feeling crowd and yet distrustful of the crowd; suspicious of our own unleashed grief.

It was impossible not to be profoundly moved by the murder of Jessica and Holly, or gripped by the narrative that unfolded in the small English village. Some stories have a particular resonance; like tuning forks they set up a ringing vibration in our own lives. But that does not mean they have a particular meaning.

What lesson can we learn from the short lives and sudden deaths of Jessica Chapman and Holly Wells? What lesson from Ian Huntley's unnoticed spiral into brutality? What lesson from Maxine Carr's blindness? The real meaning of Soham lies in the way we responded to it – with hysteria and terror and an euphoria of sadness; with sentimentality, acute empathy and a collective mourning that was like a spasm of religious fervour in our post-secular age. The touching pair of ten-year-old girls, with their radiant faces and their trusting gaze, became a revered symbol of childhood and of innocence betrayed; onto that tiny and yet extraordinarily robust icon, we let all our fears and sorrows settle for a while. But we're fickle creatures.

The grief – sincere and yet not entirely authentic, whole-hearted and yet a far cry from broken-hearted – was like a contagion, and then we recovered because, after all, it was just something in the air we breathed. There will always be new passing viruses, different stories to send that ripple down our spine, adored strangers to mourn, other victims who strike the right note at the right time, and who come to stand for something larger than themselves, just for a while.

Just for a while, Jessica and Holly haunted us; enchanting ghosts in our midst. For a while we couldn't let them go. Now they've faded, and the grief remains where it always belonged: with the family who loved them and will be haunted forever. The clock that could not be turned forward, ticking on. Fourteen minutes to seven, on the damp evening of Sunday August fourth. The clock stopped.